'This is an engrossing, persuasiv … introduction to diverse ways in which scholars have interpreted the New Testament in relation to anti-Judaism. It's a must-read for anyone who wishes to understand what is at stake in the debate, and how and why it matters. Donaldson's excellent book will surely lay the groundwork for future discussions of this important topic.'

Adele Reinhartz, Professor
Department of Classics and Religion
University of Ottawa

'Donaldson is an internationally recognized interpreter of the New Testament and the Judaism in which it emerged. In this meticulous and nuanced study, he analyses key New Testament texts to see whether or to what extent anti-semitism is present. He concludes that in interpreting the New Testament an awareness of the history of scriptural interpretation and its effects on others, particularly Jews, must form an integral part of the process. An excellent and much-needed introduction to a difficult subject that will enrich scholars, students and the general reader.'

William S. Campbell
Reader in Biblical Studies
University of Wales Lampeter

'This is a sensitive, level-headed approach to a tension-filled topic that will appeal to all readers of goodwill, whatever their religious persuasions or lack of them. Donaldson defuses stereotypes and caricatures by focusing on the complexities of key New Testament texts. Particularly striking is his conclusion that the canon of the New Testament offers more options for Christian self-definition today in relation to Judaism than the compilers of the canon themselves were able to utilize.'

John Koenig
Glorvina Rossell Hoffman Professor of New Testament
The General Theological Seminary, New York

'In this perceptive and engaging guide, Donaldson skilfully analyses New Testament texts that could be considered anti-Jewish in relation to a diversity of interpretations, demonstrating that interpretative decisions have moral implications that cannot be neglected. His own constructive proposals can only enhance responsible engagement with scriptural texts in today's complex world of faith.'

Bruce W. Longenecker
Professor of Religion and W. W. Melton Chair
Baylor University

'Donaldson's study is a judicious and balanced treatment of one of the most difficult issues in New Testament interpretation.'

Robert Jewett
Guest Professor of New Testament
University of Heidelberg

Terence L. Donaldson is the Lord and Lady Coggan Professor of New Testament Studies at Wycliffe College, an Anglican seminary within the Toronto School of Theology and the University of Toronto. Currently, he also serves as the Director of Advanced Degree Programs at the Toronto School of Theology. He is particularly interested in the theological status of Gentiles within both Second-Temple Judaism and early Christianity. His published work in this area includes books on Matthew (*Jesus on the Mountain* (1985)), Paul (*Paul and the Gentiles* (1997)) and Second-Temple Judaism (*Judaism and the Gentiles: Patterns of Universalism (to 135* CE*)* (2007)).

To my colleagues in the Canadian Society of Biblical Studies, especially Peter Richardson and Steve Wilson

JEWS AND ANTI-JUDAISM IN THE NEW TESTAMENT

Decision points and divergent interpretations

TERENCE L. DONALDSON

BAYLOR UNIVERSITY PRESS

First published in Great Britain in 2010 by
Society for Promoting Christian Knowledge
36 Causton Street
London SW1P 4ST

and in the United States of America in 2010 by
Baylor University Press, Waco, Texas 76798-7363

Copyright © Terence L. Donaldson 2010

All rights reserved. No part of this book may be reproduced or transmitted in any form or by any means, electronic or mechanical, including photocopying, recording, or by any information storage and retrieval system, without permission in writing from the publisher.

SPCK does not necessarily endorse the individual views contained in its publications.

The author and publisher have made every effort to ensure that the external website and email addresses included in this book are correct and up to date at the time of going to press. The author and publisher are not responsible for the content, quality or continuing accessibility of the sites.

Unless otherwise indicated, Scripture quotations are the author's own translation. Scripture quotations marked NRSV are taken from the New Revised Standard Version of the Bible, Anglicized Edition, copyright © 1989, 1995 by the Division of Christian Education of the National Council of the Churches of Christ in the USA. Used by permission. All rights reserved.

British Library Cataloguing-in-Publication Data
A catalogue record for this book is available from the British Library

SPCK ISBN 978–0–281–05883–9

Library of Congress Cataloging-in-Publication Data is on file at
the Library of Congress, Washington, DC

Baylor ISBN 978–1–60258–263–7

1 3 5 7 9 10 8 6 4 2

Typeset by Graphicraft Ltd, Hong Kong
Printed in Great Britain by Ashford Colour Press

Produced on paper from sustainable forests

Contents

Preface

In the first year of my theological studies, curious about the rapid transformation of early Christianity from a Jewish messianic movement to a Gentile religion, I stumbled across James Parkes's *The Conflict of the Church and the Synagogue*, a prescient work published in 1934, one year after Hitler came to power. Parkes was an Anglican priest who had become absorbed with the issue of antisemitism while working in refugee relief following the First World War. His quest for the origins of the kind of antisemitic attitudes that were prevalent in Europe led him to an exploration of Christian teaching about the Jews, and eventually led him back to the writings of the apologists and early church fathers. Under his guidance I read for the first time the *adversus Judaeos* writings of the early Church (writings 'against the Jews') and saw how this tradition, forged as an apologetic device to help the Church make its way in the Roman world, fostered anti-Jewish attitudes within Christianity that eventually contributed to the rise of antisemitism.

Parkes's book had a profoundly unsettling effect on me, in part because it raised questions about the New Testament itself. Parkes served for me as a stepping-stone to other authors who were wrestling with the depiction of Jews and Judaism in the New Testament, including Jules Isaac, Gregory Baum and Rosemary Ruether. This early experience had the effect of raising for me a set of scholarly questions that have absorbed me ever since.

Through the years I have explored these questions in courses that I have offered on a regular basis – 'New Testament Thought in Holocaust Perspective' in an earlier period, and more recently a graduate seminar 'Early Christian Self-definition and the Separation from Judaism'. My purpose in these courses has been not so much to argue for a particular position, as to lead students into the issues and to help them become aware both of the range of scholarly opinion and of the exegetical decision points that led to differing interpretations. Not coincidentally, this is also the purpose of this book. While I hope that it will be read by some of my scholarly colleagues, I have written it primarily for students and others who might be interested in an entry-level treatment, to provide them with an introduction to these issues and with tools and insights that will enable them to wrestle with the pertinent New Testament material on their own.

Scriptural citations are taken from the New Revised Standard Version where indicated; where citations differ from the NRSV, in the interest of clarity or of the argument at hand, the rendering is my own.

In keeping with the purpose of the book, I have tried to keep footnotes and references to secondary material to a minimum. If the index of modern authors at the end of the book were instead a list of scholars from whom I have learned much and to whom I am therefore indebted, it would be a much longer list indeed. I trust that any colleagues whose names would have appeared in such a list may discern the points at which my indebtedness to them is apparent.

In addition, I need to acknowledge a number of more specific debts. I express my thanks here to students in Saskatoon and Toronto who have taken my two courses over the years, and who have helped to sharpen my thinking and to shape the substance of this book; to Sherri Trautwein, a doctoral student at the Toronto School of Theology, who has checked all of the secondary references, saving me from a number of embarrassments, and has prepared the indexes; to the colleagues who read the manuscript in its pre-publication form and have been generous with both their time and their assessments; to Rebecca Mulhearn and Carey Newman, together with their co-workers at SPCK and Baylor University Press respectively, for the care with which they have guided the manuscript through the editorial and publication process.

Finally, I want to express my gratitude to my colleagues in the Canadian Society of Biblical Studies. Four years after my initial encounter with the work of James Parkes, I attended my first CSBS meeting and discovered the seminar 'Anti-Judaism in Early Christianity', then in its third year. I knew immediately that this was a society in which I could find an academic home, which it has proved to be through the thirty years since this first encounter. I am grateful for the rich contribution that the society has made to my scholarly life over these years. Accordingly, as an expression of gratitude I dedicate this book to the members of the CSBS – especially Peter Richardson and Steve Wilson, who have been mentors, colleagues and friends, and to whom I owe a considerable intellectual and professional debt.

1

Introduction

Antisemitism and the New Testament
The question raised

In 1948, in a period when the full extent of Hitler's 'final solution' had just recently come to light and when victors and vanquished alike had been brought face to face with the horrors that had taken place in the heart of Christian Europe, a book appeared that sensitive Christians found to be deeply disturbing, as it raised questions that went to the heart of Christian faith and self-identity. The author was Jules Isaac, a 71-year-old French historian of Jewish descent; the book was entitled simply *Jésus et Israël*.[1]

When war broke out in 1939, Jules Isaac was at the peak of a brilliant academic career. Raised in a military family and a decorated veteran of the First World War, he had trained as a historian, subsequently becoming a prominent academic and author of a seven-volume history that served as a standard textbook for high school and university students. In 1936 he was appointed by the French government as the Inspector General of Education for the nation as a whole. While Jewishness was part of his identity, he was an ideal example of the social emancipation that European Jews had enjoyed in the nineteenth and early twentieth centuries.

Things changed quickly with the Nazi occupation of France. Deprived of his position in 1940 because he was Jewish, Isaac became increasingly concerned with a need to understand the roots of antisemitism. While he fully recognized that Nazism was not Christian, he also was aware that Hitler was able to carry out his antisemitic policies only because of an antipathy to Jews and Judaism that was deeply rooted in European culture and that had been fertilized and

[1] Jules Isaac, *Jésus et Israël* (Paris: Albin Michel, 1948); ET *Jesus and Israel* (New York: Holt, Rinehart & Winston, 1971).

nurtured through centuries of Christian teaching and worship. In 1943 his wife and several other members of his family were arrested and sent to the concentration camps, where all but his youngest son eventually perished. Shortly before her death his wife was able to send him a note: 'Save yourself for your work; the world is waiting for it.' An order was given for his arrest as well, and he spent the remainder of the war fleeing from the Nazis, hiding in various safe houses and working on his manuscript all the while.[2] When it was eventually published, it bore the inscription:

> IN MEMORIAM
> To my wife and my daughter
> Martyrs
> Killed by Hitler's Nazis[3]
> Killed
> Simply because their name was
> ISAAC

Jésus et Israël was certainly not a model of dispassionate scholarly discourse. Deeply passionate in its tone and somewhat untidy in its form, it shows the marks of having been written in anguish and on the run. But perhaps for these very reasons the book had an immediate and widespread impact. Isaac's method was simply to compare the text of the New Testament (primarily the Gospels) with later Christian commentaries on the text. His findings were that Christian interpreters, from the church fathers down to the present, systematically interpreted the New Testament according to a set of anti-Jewish themes that were widely shared by interpreters but not really supported by the Scriptures themselves. In a subsequent work he described these themes as the 'teaching of contempt' and summarized them under three headings: the degenerate state of Judaism at the time of Jesus; the collective Jewish guilt for the crime of deicide; and the dispersion

---

[2] For a brief biography, see Claire Huchet Bishop's introduction in Jules Isaac, *The Teaching of Contempt: Christian Roots of Anti-Semitism* (New York: Holt, Rinehart & Winston, 1964), 3–15.

[3] Actually, in the first edition the inscription read, 'Tuées par les Allemands'; he subsequently changed this to avoid doing to the Germans what he felt that Christian tradition had unjustly done to the Jews – ascribing guilt to a whole people.

of the Jewish people as divine punishment for this crime.[4] In *Jésus et Israël* he set out the results of his study in 21 propositions, in which he stressed the Jewishness of Jesus and of the early Church; argued for the vigour and spiritual vitality of first-century Judaism; denied that the Jewish people as a whole rejected Jesus and were responsible for his death; and argued that the diaspora was an accomplished fact long before the time of Jesus.

Isaac did not see himself as calling authentic Christianity into question. By pointing to the large gulf that existed between the historical situation apparent in the New Testament and the tendentious interpretation carried out by later commentators, he understood himself to be demonstrating that this later interpretation was 'contrary to the truth and love of him who was the Jew Jesus' and felt that he was offering 'true Christians' the opportunity of 'a profound spiritual and religious renewal'.[5]

At the same time, however, it was readily apparent that he was laying a major proportion of the blame for the Holocaust at the doorstep of the Church: 'The German responsibility for these crimes, as overwhelming as it has been, is only a derivative responsibility, grafted like a most hideous parasite on a centuries-old tradition which is a Christian tradition.'[6] Further, and closer to the concerns of this book, it was also apparent that in his view the New Testament was not fully to be exonerated.

For example, he takes great exception to the pejorative use of 'the Jews' in the Fourth Gospel, concluding that the evangelist wrote with the intention 'to treat the Jewish people as aliens, and even more as an enemy, to mark their name with a sort of brand' and to lead his Christian readers to 'be revolted by this infernal hatred'.[7] Further, he objects to the way in which all four Gospels minimize Pilate's role in what is after all a Roman execution, instead ascribing responsibility to the Jews and their leaders. He depicts the writers of these tendentious accounts as being engaged in a 'real competition to see who will make the Jews more odious', but he awards the dubious prize to the author

[4] Isaac, *Teaching of Contempt*.
[5] Isaac, *Jesus and Israel*, 400.
[6] Ibid., 399–400.
[7] Ibid., 113, 116.

of Matthew 27.25, a verse in which 'all the people', assuming the responsibility that Pilate has just declined, declare together: 'his blood be on us and on our children'. He describes this 'atrocious verse'[8] as 'a poisoned arrow, permanently embedded' in the corporate history of the Jewish people but originally fired by the 'sure hand' of Matthew himself.[9] In his view, these and other aspects of the Gospels reflect the fact that they were written in a period after the Jewish war with Rome (66–70 CE) when the Church was engaged in a painful process of separation from the synagogue.[10]

Thus even though Isaac felt that he was attacking something other than Christian faith in its essence, he nevertheless raised significant questions about the core documents of the faith. The vast gulf that he claimed to perceive lies not so much between the New Testament and later commentators as between Jesus and his later anti-Jewish interpreters, the earliest of whom, he believed, are to be found among the New Testament authors themselves. The harsh critical light that he shone on Christian antisemitism also served to cast dark shadows across at least some pages of the Christian Scriptures.

This point was not lost on his Christian readers, among whom one of the most astute was Gregory Baum, the author of the first full-scale discussion of the issues raised by *Jésus et Israël*.[11] Baum's life paralleled that of Isaac in some ways. He was of partial Jewish descent, having been born (in Berlin in 1923) into a mixed family (his mother was Jewish, his father Protestant), which meant that he too was a product of European emancipation. Like Isaac, his family was tossed about by the ill-winds of the Nazi regime; his mother perished in Berlin in 1943, while he himself fled to England as a teenager in 1939 and eventually ended up in an internment camp for German nationals in Canada. Unlike Isaac, however, he converted to Roman Catholicism and became a priest.

[8] Ibid., 328.

[9] Ibid., 338.

[10] Ibid., 294.

[11] In the preface to his 1955 book *Antisémitisme et mystère d'Israël* (Paris: A. Michel), Fadiey Lovsky made reference to the influence that *Jésus et Israël* had had on his thinking. Still, he also indicated that his book had first been written prior to the appearance of Isaac's work, so that while he had revised some of it for this publication, it by no means represented a Christian response to Isaac.

With his conversion, he also took over unquestioningly the traditional Christian attitudes towards the Jews. Referring to some talks that he was asked to give concerning the Church and the Jews, he said:

> Thus I repeated, without the slightest hesitation, the ancient stories that the Jews have been rejected and the Gentiles chosen, that the younger brother has been preferred to the older, Isaac to Ishmael, Jacob to Esau, yes, and even Abel to Cain. The Jews, I then thought – and said, in the talks which I gave – are in the likeness of Cain, a people condemned for murder . . . Without realising the implications of remarks of this kind, and the impact they make on human relations, I repeated the long litany of theological legends with which the mystery of Israel has been surrounded in the literature of the centuries.

But then, he said, he happened to read Isaac's *Jésus et Israël* and was 'shattered'.[12] Deeply affected by 'the power of Jules Isaac's book', he came to recognize 'the weak foundation this way [of characterizing the Jews] had in the gospel and the consequences it had in the domain of human relations'.[13] Consequently he embarked on a re-evaluation of his own views, the result of which appeared in 1961 as *The Jews and the Gospel.*[14]

Despite the impact of Isaac's book on his own thinking about Christian traditions, however, Baum disagreed in part with Isaac's treatment of the Gospels. He took issue with Isaac's claim 'that in the gospels themselves as we now possess them we detect a polemical bias against the Jews and unhistorical additions to discredit the people as a whole'.[15] He wrote his own book, then, 'in partial criticism' of Isaac and with the intention of showing

> that there is no foundation for the accusation that a seed of contempt and hatred for the Jews can be found in the New Testament. The final redaction of some of the books of the New Testament may bear the marks of conflict between the young Church and the Synagogue,

[12] This and the previous quotation are from Gregory Baum, *The Jews and the Gospel: A Re-Examination of the New Testament* (Westminster, Md.: Newman Press, 1961), 1.

[13] Ibid., 4.

[14] The book was re-published a few years later, with slight revisions, as *Is the New Testament Anti-Semitic? A Re-Examination of the New Testament* (Glen Rock, NJ: Paulist Press, 1965). For the revisions, see below, n. 19.

[15] Baum, *The Jews and the Gospel*, 4.

> but no degradation of the Jewish people, no unjust accusation, no malevolent prophecy is ever suggested or implied.[16]

To establish this conclusion Baum looked in detail at contentious passages in the four Gospels, Acts and Paul. While he recognized that these passages could be read in anti-Jewish ways, his general argument was that this can take place only when the texts are read without historical awareness, so that later developments come to be read back into them. He argued that the New Testament writers understood the Christian movement to have emerged as the result of an 'eschatological [i.e. end-times] schism' that had been precipitated within the Jewish people by the messianic ministry of Jesus; that this schism was in accordance with the expectation of Israel's prophets; that early Christian polemic is best understood as belonging to the same category as the denunciations of Israel carried out by the prophets; and that the community of salvation resulting from this schism is to be seen as Israel in its truest form, a new community that continues to be open to Jews even as it incorporates Gentiles.

Baum's argument, however, depends on a distinction between 'the Jewish people' and 'Judaism' that many (including eventually Baum himself) would perceive to be too fine to be helpful. In his view the Gospels are not anti-Jewish, because it was '[t]he Judaism which rejected Christ [that] was reprobated, not the Jews'.[17] To say this, however, is in effect to assign reprobation to all those Jews who continue to identify themselves in terms of this Judaism, for it is clear from his emphasis on conversion that what is reprobated is not an abstract religion but the people who adhere to it. To say that the Gospels are not anti-Jewish because they continue to invite Jews to believe in Jesus would provide small comfort to the great majority of Jews, those who continue to identify themselves in terms of a Judaism that belongs to what Baum characterized as 'an old order' that has 'passed and been replaced by the gospel', and in terms of a law that Christ, by fulfilling it, has rendered 'void of meaning'.[18]

---

[16] Ibid., 4, 5. He sets out two additional purposes: to defend the Jews against the misinterpretations of the New Testament in Christian tradition; and to refute those Christians who, though well-meaning, were compromising the Catholic faith in their attempts to make reparations to the Jews.

[17] Ibid., 55.

[18] Ibid., 54, 58.

Baum's thinking continued to develop, however,[19] partly under the influence of Rosemary Ruether. Invited to write an introduction to her important work *Faith and Fratricide*, published in 1974, he used the occasion to express his agreement with her analysis and to declare that his earlier book 'no longer represents my position on the relationship between Church and Synagogue'.[20]

Faith and Fratricide was sweeping in its scope and shattering in its conclusions. In successive chapters Ruether dealt with the place of Jews and Judaism in the Graeco-Roman world, the anti-Judaism of the New Testament, the development of 'the negative myth of the Jews' in the church fathers, and the social incorporation of this negative myth in Christendom from Constantine through to the modern period. She was unflinching in her rejection of attempts to erect a protective barrier around the New Testament, both those that looked for a contrast between the New Testament itself and its later, largely Gentile, interpreters, and those that would locate the roots of later Christian antisemitism in pre-existing Graeco-Roman attitudes towards Jews and Judaism.[21] She argued instead that Christian anti-Judaism (which inevitably expressed itself as antisemitism whenever the Church had sufficient social and political power) was intrinsic to the christological message that was part of the Christian movement from the beginning.

The heart and start of the problem, in her view, is that the early Church wanted both to identify Jesus as the Messiah and to authenticate this claim on the basis of (what the Church eventually came

---

19 Some changes are apparent even in the second edition of his work (*Is the New Testament Anti-Semitic?*). For example, he removes a statement expressing support for a mission to Jewish people and the possibility of conversion (pp. 326–7) and he adds a concluding paragraph in which he asserts that New Testament statements about the Church and Judaism apply to the first-century context and cannot simply be transferred to the present day (pp. 347–8).

20 Rosemary R. Ruether, *Faith and Fratricide: The Theological Roots of Anti-Semitism* (Minneapolis: Seabury, 1974), 4.

21 This latter approach was taken by Lovsky (*Antisémitisme et mystère d'Israël*) and also by Marcel Simon, who responded to Isaac in the second edition of his *Verus Israel: A Study of the Relations Between Christians and Jews in the Roman Empire (135–425)* (New York: Oxford University Press for the Littman Library, 1986), first published (in French) in 1948. See also Edward H. Flannery, *The Anguish of the Jews: Twenty-Three Centuries of Anti-Semitism* (New York: Macmillan, 1965), 60–1.

to call) the Old Testament. Since Jews also claimed these Scriptures as divine revelation but at the same time refused to believe in Jesus, the early Christians found that in order to proclaim their message (that the crucified and resurrected Jesus was the promised Messiah) they simultaneously had to refute the Jewish interpretation and to claim these Scriptures as their own exclusive possession. Anti-Judaism arises, then, as the 'left hand of Christology':

> What we have here are two sides of the same argument. On the one hand, the Church argues that the true meaning of the Scriptures is that of a prophecy of Jesus as the Christ. And, on the other hand, it developed a collection of texts 'against the Jews' to show why the authority of the official Jewish tradition should be discounted when it refutes this christological midrash of its own Scriptures.[22]

Consequently she concludes that '[t]here is no way to rid Christianity of its anti-Judaism, which constantly takes social expression in anti-Semitism, without grappling finally with its christological hermeneutic itself'.[23] In a final chapter she engages in such a 'grappling', partly (as Baum points out) by using the traditional idea of the 'second coming', with its implication that Jesus' messianic role is unfinished and yet to be fulfilled, as a way of undercutting any premature Christian claims to finality and thus of opening up some theological breathing space for Jews and Judaism.

Faith and Fratricide turned out to be something of a watershed. While significant discussion continues to take place concerning the New Testament and anti-Judaism, some of which will be reflected in the pages to follow, there has been little attempt since then to place this issue in the context of such a comprehensive treatment. My purpose here in any case is not to provide a full history of the discussion, but to use a few selected works to introduce the issue. Before moving on, however, it is appropriate to mention one other author, who in a way provides a set of bookends to the history from Isaac to Ruether.

The first full-scale attempt to take up Ruether's challenge was a volume of essays edited by Alan T. Davies, *Antisemitism and the*

---

22 Ruether, *Faith and Fratricide*, 65.
23 Ibid., 116.

Foundations of Christianity.[24] Appearing in 1979, the volume was dedicated to James Parkes, who also wrote a preface to the work. In his own introduction, Davies acknowledged that '[w]e who think and speak on this subject today are in one way or another all his debtors'.[25]

James Parkes, who at the time of writing was in his early eighties (he died in 1981), had been absorbed with the question of antisemitism and its origins since 1925 when, as an Anglican priest and under the auspices of the Student Christian Movement, he was engaged in relief work in post-war Europe. In his first published work on the topic,[26] he traced the phenomenon back to the Jewish massacres that were carried out by those on their way to the first crusade in 1096. Puzzled by what seemed to be a sudden outbreak of violence, he decided to do a more thorough investigation as a doctoral thesis. The result was published in 1934 as *The Conflict of the Church and the Synagogue: A Study in the Origins of Antisemitism*.[27]

Written while the Nazi storm-clouds were massing on the horizon, the book was ahead of its time and its real significance was not fully recognized until later. Like Ruether, Parkes provided a comprehensive survey that moved from the situation of Jews in the Roman world, through the New Testament period and the subsequent development of 'an official attitude'[28] towards Judaism by the church fathers, and on to the progressively worsening situation of the Jewish people in Christian society from Constantine onwards. Like Ruether, Parkes traced the origins of European antisemitism back to the social legislation of the Christian Roman empire and, behind that, to the theological polemic forged in the second and third centuries (the *adversus Judaeos* tradition; i.e. writings 'against the Jews') – and not to the anti-Jewish attitudes that were already present in the

[24] *Antisemitism and the Foundations of Christianity* (New York and Toronto: Paulist Press, 1979).

[25] Ibid., xvi.

[26] James Parkes, *The Jew and His Neighbour: A Study of the Causes of Anti-Semitism* (London: SCM Press, 1930).

[27] *The Conflict of the Church and the Synagogue: A Study in the Origins of Antisemitism* (London: Soncino Press, 1934).

[28] Ibid., 95.

Graeco-Roman world. Like Isaac,[29] he believed that the war with Rome precipitated a 'parting of the ways'[30] and with it a significant shift in Christian attitudes towards its parent religion. Thus, like Isaac, he felt that some aspects of the New Testament, notably the Gospel of John, were tainted by anti-Judaic attitudes characteristic of the later period.[31]

Questions raised by Parkes, Isaac, Baum, Ruether and others continue to be pressing ones in New Testament interpretation, especially for the Church and those who identify with the Christian tradition. The primary reason for this continues to be the lingering nightmare of the Holocaust and the painful recognition of Christian complicity in the environment that made it possible. Several other factors, however, have had a part to play in shaping the ongoing discussion.

One is the significant cultural change that has taken place in the formerly Christian societies of North America and Europe since the end of the Second World War. The waning of Christendom, the globalization of culture and the increasingly pluralistic character of western society add another dimension of difficulty to texts that apparently seek to advance Christian claims by denigrating Jews and denouncing Judaism.

Another factor is the phenomenon of a growing interaction between Jewish and Christian scholars. What is important here is not only the Jewish–Christian dialogue generally, but more specifically an increasingly collegial interaction among scholars with a common interest in questions of origin – that is, questions concerning the process by which Christianity and rabbinic Judaism emerged out of a common Jewish matrix in the later Second-Temple period. To a certain extent this engagement was under way well before the Holocaust, with scholars such as Claude Montefiore, Solomon Schechter and Joseph Klausner on the Jewish side, and, on the Christian, James Parkes

---

[29] Isaac subsequently acknowledged the importance of Parkes's work and expressed regret that he did not know of it when he was doing his own work; see *Jesus and Israel*, 240.

[30] The title of ch. 3.

[31] *The Conflict of the Church and the Synagogue*, 82–4. See also his *Jesus, Paul and the Jews* (London: SCM Press, 1936), where he defends Jesus and Paul (in contrast to post-70 CE figures and authors) from the charge of antisemitism.

and George Foot Moore. In the quarter-century between *Jésus et Israël* and *Faith and Fratricide*, this Jewish enterprise was carried on by Samuel Sandmel, E. R. Goodenough, Geza Vermes, Hans-Joachim Schoeps, David Flusser and others, and since then many others have taken up the task (e.g. Alan Segal, Daniel Boyarin, Mark Nanos, Adele Reinhartz, Paula Fredriksen, Amy-Jill Levine). For their part, Christian scholars have increasingly abandoned defensive apologetic and have been willing to incorporate into their own work a sympathetic awareness of how Christian origins look from the perspective of informed Jewish observers.

A third factor has to do with advances in our understanding of Judaism in the first century, which have given us much clearer insights into the social location of early Jewish Christianity and into the process by which the Christian movement separated from Judaism and developed into a Gentile religion. One important catalyst here was the discovery of the Dead Sea Scrolls in 1947 (coincidentally, just prior to the publication of Isaac's book). These writings have led to a greater appreciation of the diversity of Second-Temple Judaism – both directly, by providing primary evidence for a hitherto little-known group,[32] and indirectly, by encouraging scholars to take more seriously the evidence for diversity in already known Jewish sources. Prior to this it had been possible to conceive of Judaism as a monolithic entity, from which Christianity was categorically distinct from the outset; or as dominated by a 'normative' form, in contrast to various marginal groups of which early Christianity was one; or as characterized by contrasting pairs of broad tendencies (e.g. legalistic and apocalyptic; Palestinian and diaspora/Hellenistic), with one leading to rabbinic Judaism and the other to Christianity. Since then, however, it has become increasingly apparent that earliest Christianity needs to be seen as part of the diversity of the Second-Temple period, as one of a number of Jewish groups competing for status and influence within a larger diversity. We will return to this issue in more detail below.

Diversity is a characteristic not only of Second-Temple Judaism, however, but also of the phenomenon under discussion in this

[32] Assuming that those responsible for the scrolls were related in some way to the Essenes described by Josephus, Philo and Pliny the Elder.

book – namely, scholarly opinion concerning the New Testament and anti-Judaism. The range of opinion observed among the scholars discussed to this point has been replicated, extended and given greater nuance in the ongoing scholarly discussion and debate. The purpose of this book is to provide an introduction to the scholarly discussion of the questions raised by Parkes, Isaac, Baum, Ruether and others, and to the range of approaches that have been taken. Thus my goal is not to argue for a particular approach or set of answers, but, generally speaking, to introduce readers to the questions and the way they have been treated. More specifically, it will be my goal to drill down to the New Testament itself, describing how individual texts have been interpreted in different ways and attempting to show how different interpretations have been generated by differences in assumption, approach and method.

Given the introductory nature and limited scope of this book, it will not be possible to provide a comprehensive treatment of the topic or to deal with all of the New Testament passages that pertain to it. I will devote individual chapters to the New Testament writings that are most significant for the topic – Matthew, Luke–Acts, John and the letters of Paul – and discuss the remaining writings more briefly in another chapter. In each case I will begin with an egregious text, aspect or theme, one that has most often been labelled anti-Judaic and that has figured prominently in the discussion. In the chapter on Matthew, for example, the cry of 'all the people' in 27.25 is an obvious choice. I will then identify a representative range of interpretations, attempting as far as possible to begin with the work of Parkes, Isaac, Baum and Ruether, before moving on to more recent discussion. Then I will endeavour to show how these various interpretations have arisen, looking at the text itself, its context in the work as a whole and the set of interpretive decisions that have to be made in each case. In a final chapter I will exchange the role of sideline observer for that of an on-field participant, providing some comment of my own on the discussion surveyed in the previous chapters.

The question examined

Before turning to the New Testament directly, however, we should give some consideration to the terms in which the question has been posed. In part, this has to do with terminology (e.g. antisemitism, anti-Judaism), though this leads into larger issues concerning the categories within which the discussion has been carried out. The purpose of what follows is not to arrive at definitive answers to the four questions that are posed but, instead, to analyse the questions in order to identify distinctions and categories that will help us as we turn to the scholarly interpretation of the New Testament itself.

Is the New Testament antisemitic?

The term 'anti-Semitism' was first used in the context of specious racial theories that emerged in France and Germany in the latter part of the nineteenth century.[33] Borrowing a term used by linguists in their classification of languages into Semitic (Hebrew, Aramaic, Syriac, Arabic) and Indo-European or Aryan (Sanskrit, Greek, Latin, German and others), 'race theorists' such as Wilhelm Marr argued for the superiority of the 'Aryan race' over the 'Semitic', though for all practical purposes the latter term referred exclusively to Jews. Marr and those like him proudly declared themselves to be anti-Semites; only after the Nazi period did the term take on its strictly pejorative sense.

Given these origins, some have argued that the term should not be used at all, since it is inaccurate (it has to do with Jews, not any larger group of 'Semites') and ill-founded (on discredited pseudo-scientific race theories).[34] Nevertheless, the phenomenon is real and the term is too well established to expect that it might be replaced. Most scholars continue to use it, though some prefer the unhyphenated form 'antisemitism', as a way of distancing the term from the discredited theories associated with its original formulation.[35]

But can the term be applied to the New Testament? This depends on the definition of antisemitism, and here various suggestions have been made about how antisemitism might be differentiated from other, less extreme phenomena. Some of these have to do with

[33] See the discussion in Parkes, *The Conflict of the Church and the Synagogue*, xv–xvi.

[34] See e.g. George M. Smiga, *Pain and Polemic: Anti-Judaism in the Gospels* (New York: Paulist Press, 1992), 11.

[35] Parkes has used the unhyphenated form consistently, treating it as an English equivalent of *Judenhass* (hatred of Jews); see Davies, *Antisemitism and the Foundations of Christianity*, viii.

(1) the subject (the identity of those who hold certain opinions, engage in certain forms of speech or carry out certain actions), others with (2) the object (the target towards which such opinions, speech or actions are directed, i.e. the identity of the group or entity to which they refer), and still others with (3) the intention (the end to which such speech or actions are directed).

With respect to the first category, some scholars see antisemitic opinions, speech or actions as something necessarily restricted to Gentile outsiders,[36] which means that the term could not apply to most of the New Testament authors. With respect to the second, some differentiate between race and religion, restricting 'antisemitism' to opinions, speech or actions directed at Jews as a race or ethnic group, and using some other term (often anti-Judaism) to describe opinions or actions directed against members of a specific religion. On the basis of such a definition, Nazism was antisemitic in a way that, say, medieval Christendom was not, in that under the Nazis someone with Jewish ancestry could not gain exemption from anti-Jewish policies through conversion or assimilation. Also within the second category are those who make a distinction between attitudes, speech and actions directed towards Jews as a distinct people or social group, and criticisms of the beliefs and practices of a particular religion. Edward Flannery, for example, sees anti-Judaism as distinct from antisemitism in that it 'is purely theological; it rejects Judaism as a way of salvation but not the Jews as a people'.[37] This distinction between religion and people readily slides over into the third, which has to do with distinctions between various purposes to which anti-Jewish discourse or actions might be directed. One form of this is a differentiation between religious or theological *apologetic*, discourse whose purpose is to solidify the self-identity of Christians or to attract potential converts (Jewish or Gentile), and social *polemic*, discourse designed to denigrate Jewish people themselves.[38] Another is a differentiation that would restrict the use of 'antisemitism' to the social

[36] E.g. John G. Gager, *The Origins of Anti-Semitism* (Oxford: Oxford University Press, 1983), 8.

[37] Flannery, *The Anguish of the Jews*, 60; see also his 'Anti-Judaism and Anti-Semitism: A Necessary Distinction', *Journal of Ecumenical Studies* 10 (1973): 581–8.

[38] In Flannery's opinion, for discourse to be antisemitic, it 'must include a note of hatred or contempt of the *Jewish people as such*' (italics his); 'Anti-Judaism and Anti-Semitism', 583.

and political realm, especially to actions taken by the state or by other groups with sufficient social power to translate anti-Judaic attitudes into legal codes or social policy. Thus Ruether can speak of Christian 'anti-Judaism' as something that 'constantly takes social expression in anti-Semitism'.[39]

On the basis of such distinctions, one could argue – and many have – that the New Testament cannot be described as antisemitic. Even so, however, the term cannot be fully excluded from the discussion. Even if this argument should be valid within the fairly narrow historical context of the original authors and their intended readers, the question of antisemitism arises only because these writings were taken up into the canon of (1) a largely Gentile Church, where they have functioned (2) to inculcate negative attitudes towards the Jewish people themselves and (3) have thus been a factor in the emergence of harmful social policy and state activity. Even if we can make distinctions that allow us to absolve the New Testament itself from the charge of antisemitism, these same distinctions require us to recognize that the New Testament has been interpreted in antisemitic ways and made to serve antisemitic purposes. Unless we are interested solely in historical questions and not in ongoing hermeneutical significance, the term cannot be excluded from the discussion.

Is the New Testament anti-Judaic?

If the New Testament is not antisemitic, especially in its original historical context, can it nevertheless be described as anti-Judaic? As we have seen, some prefer to cast the question in these terms on the grounds that 'anti-Judaism' highlights the theological and hermeneutical character of the early Christian stance towards Jews and Judaism. In this view, 'antisemitism' in the ancient world is more appropriately reserved for those Greeks and Romans whose negative opinions, speech and actions were directed towards Jews as an ethnic entity. As Gager puts it, the Christian phenomenon is 'of a different order'; 'Christian anti-Judaism is primarily a matter of religious and theological disagreement'.[40] For Flannery, there is a 'necessary distinction'[41] between the two.

[39] Ruether, *Faith and Fratricide*, 116.

[40] Gager, *The Origins of Anti-Semitism*, 8.

[41] The subtitle of his article 'Anti-Judaism and Anti-Semitism'.

Others, however, argue that even this term is inappropriate for the New Testament. Most of the New Testament writers were native-born Jews who saw themselves as part of the faithful remnant of Jewish tradition in their own day. How could a Jew such as Matthew or Paul be described as anti-Judaic? In support of this position appeal is often made to two phenomena within the Jewish world and tradition. One is the self-critical stance of the prophets. Baum, for example, argues that both Jesus and Matthew drew on 'the traditional language of the Hebrew prophets' to castigate their contemporaries, and with a purpose similar to that of the prophets – to call their own people to repentance and conversion. It is a mistake to confuse 'prophetic indignation' with 'anti-Jewish feeling'.[42] A second appeal, more contemporaneous with the New Testament, has to do with the existence of other Jewish groups or sects that stood in opposition to the more mainstream forms of Judaism. A prime case in point is the community that produced the Dead Sea Scrolls, commonly referred to as the Qumran community (after the modern name for the site near the Dead Sea where the scrolls were found). While the Dead Sea Scrolls have harsh things to say about the Jerusalem establishment and other members of the 'sons of darkness', one cannot describe a sect whose members were entirely Jewish as anti-Judaic. In this view, then, the New Testament authors are no more anti-Judaic than was Jeremiah or Qumran's Teacher of Righteousness.

While the argument has a certain force, it also needs to be recognized that there is a significant difference between the prophets and the Qumran community in their respective relationships to the Jewish people as a whole. The prophets primarily addressed themselves to what they saw as corruption, faithlessness and apostasy. Their goal was correction – to denounce the people for falling away from their covenantal identity and commitments, to call for repentance and to hold out the promise of divine forgiveness and blessing. The stance of the Qumran community, however, was more sectarian. This community apparently saw themselves as the sole recipients of a special revelation granted to them through the Teacher of Righteousness, and thus as the exclusive bearers of the name of Israel. Their polemic against the rest of the Jewish world served primarily

[42] Baum, *The Jews and the Gospel*, 45.

to reinforce their own self-understanding; if it had a more positive, outward purpose, it was to persuade other Jews to convert and to join the only true covenant community.[43] While perhaps neither can be described as anti-Judaic, the differences between them suggest that finer distinctions are called for.

The prophet analogy might be helpful in thinking about John the Baptist and perhaps even Jesus. But in the post-Easter situation, the relationship between the Jewish-Christian movement and the Jewish world as a whole is closer to that of the Qumran community. The early Jewish Christians were not simply trying to correct and reform a people that had gone astray from their ancestral commitments. Early Christianity was characterized by certain beliefs about Jesus, which were placed in the framework of a particular way of interpreting the Scriptures. These beliefs and this interpretive framework were certainly not shared by Judaism as a whole. Indeed, in their attempts to define and defend themselves, most early Christians seem to have been sharply critical of all other Jews who did not accept their beliefs about Jesus and the Scriptures. While they may have been more interested than the Qumran community in calling their kinsfolk to conversion, they were equally sectarian, setting themselves over against the rest of Judaism in a definitive way. But does this constitute anti-Judaism?

In one of the chapters in *Antisemitism and the Foundations of Christianity*, Douglas Hare has attempted to move the discussion forward by identifying different types of anti-Judaism.[44] 'Prophetic anti-Judaism', as its name implies, is modelled on the prophets of Israel, who denounced Israel as a whole for its lack of faithfulness to the covenant and the leaders in particular for failing in their responsibility. For Hare, both John and Jesus fall into this type. 'Jewish-Christian anti-Judaism', by contrast, emerges only after the death and resurrection of Jesus. Unlike the former, this form of anti-Judaism castigates the Jewish people not simply for its sin and unfaithfulness but also 'for refusing to acknowledge the crucial importance for salvation history of the crucified and risen Jesus'. Still, this approach

[43] The element of persuasion and conversion is more to the fore in *4QHalakhic Letter*, an early document, than in later writings.

[44] Douglas R. A. Hare, 'The Rejection of the Jews in the Synoptic Gospels and Acts', in Davies, *Antisemitism and the Foundations of Christianity*, 28–32.

continued to believe that God had not rejected Israel and that repentance and conversion were possible. The third type, 'Gentilizing anti-Judaism', is characteristic of a Church completely separate from the Jewish world, made up of Gentile outsiders along with Jews who have abandoned their Jewish identity entirely. In this type of anti-Judaism, castigation of the Jewish people no longer is directed at conversion but instead expresses the belief that 'God has finally and irrevocably rejected his people' and has chosen a new people to take Israel's place.

In order to develop this set of types further, it is useful to refer again to the categories of subject (the identity and social location of those characterized by certain opinions, speech or actions), object (the target towards which such things are directed) and intent (the end to which these things are intended to lead). In all three of Hare's types the target or object is established Jewish religion, rather than ethnic identity. Still, it would be overly simplistic to describe what we are dealing with simply as a matter of religious ideas or competing theologies. While negative attitudes, speech and action are not directed at Jews as an ethnic group, we are not dealing just with disembodied ideas or theologies. Each of these types has an intrinsic social element; they have to do with distinct groups, engaged in competition with other groups for power and influence, drawing boundaries to differentiate themselves from others, attempting to attract followers and gain support, and so on. While there is a distinction to be drawn between anti-Judaism and antisemitism, it cannot be reduced to a distinction between ideas and social conflict.

The differences among Hare's types arise from the other two categories – the social location of the subject and the intent of the 'anti-Judaic' attitudes, speech and action. With respect to social location, his three types represent distinct degrees of difference from the dominant culture. Those who engage in 'prophetic anti-Judaism' are embedded in the dominant culture, in the sense that they identify with the inherited tradition and differ from the rest of the culture only in their belief that certain others have not been sufficiently faithful to the tradition. Those who engage in 'Jewish-Christian anti-Judaism' are sectarian, interpreting the tradition in ways that set them apart from the dominant culture and understanding themselves (and those prepared to join them) to be the only legitimate continuation of the tradition. Those who engage in 'Gentilizing anti-Judaism' are completely separate from the dominant Jewish culture, interacting with it from an external perspective and social location.

With respect to intent, in each of Hare's types we can discern both inward and outward aspects to the 'anti-Judaic' activity. In each case there is an inward element, the activity in question serving to reaffirm and legitimate the self-understanding of the subject group. There is also an outward element, one that differs according to the social location of the group engaged in such activity. In the first two, the negative speech and action is directed towards a more positive goal with respect to the Jewish people as a whole: correction and renewal in the first instance, conversion and the promise of messianic blessing in the second. In the third type, there is a positive end as well, but the recipients are different: Judaism is denounced so that others (primarily Gentiles) might believe and join a group that is totally separate from the Jewish world.

What then constitutes anti-Judaism? When is the term appropriate? It certainly seems to be appropriate in the third type, where the two groups are separate and the activity in question is external to Jewish society. With respect to the first type at the other end of the spectrum, the term seems totally inappropriate; to the extent that the prophets were calling their own people back to their own fundamental commitments and identity, it is neither accurate nor helpful to call them anti-Judaic. Such self-criticism might be called anti-apostasy or anti-corruption, but not anti-Judaism. With respect to the second type, to the extent that these sects were still located within the dominant culture (even if the character of that location was a matter of dispute), anti-Judaism is not a helpful term. Neither the Qumran community nor the earliest Jewish-Christian movement was anti-Judaic. The term would not be appropriate even if such groups were to be thought of as marginal deviations from a dominant 'normative' Judaism; it would be even less appropriate if full recognition is given to the diverse character of Judaism in this period. Still, by putting themselves forward as an alternative to the rest of Judaism, such sects tended to be 'anti-the rest of Judaism', which means that they were characterized by a certain latent or potential anti-Judaism. If the separation from the larger body should increase, this potential anti-Judaism would become increasingly real, especially if the larger body should become less diverse and if the separated group began to incorporate non-Jews in significant numbers.[45]

In sum, Hare's three types should be thought of as points on a spectrum rather than as discrete alternative categories. The greater the distance in social location between the group in question and Jewish society as a whole; the greater the degree to which the target is Jewish belief and practice as a whole; the greater the element of negative intent with respect to the Jewish world (denigration, denunciation) instead of positive (correction, conversion) – the more appropriate it is to use 'anti-Judaism' as a descriptive category.

All along the spectrum, however, we are dealing not simply with ideas or theologies, but with groups and movements engaged in the process of social formation and self-definition. This leads to a third way in which the question has been posed.

Is the New Testament supersessionist?

To say that one thing supersedes another is to say that the one comes to replace the other because of the inferiority or deficiency of the latter, thus rendering it obsolete. With respect to Jewish–Christian relations, 'supersessionism' refers to the idea that the Christian Church has superseded the Israel of the 'Old Testament' – in other words, that the Church has succeeded and replaced Israel as the people of God and has inherited everything of value in Israel's tradition; that only the Christian movement has any legitimate claim to the Old Testament and the revelation it represents; that pre-Christian Israel has been rendered obsolete and that ongoing non-Christian Judaism is thus illegitimate; that Judaism has been cut off from the Scriptures and has no claim to it; and so on. While the term 'supersede' was common in an earlier era as a positive characterization of Christianity,[46] more recently it (along with the related nouns 'supersession' and

---

[45] On the basis of similar considerations, Smiga has suggested alternative designations for Hare's three categories: 'prophetic polemic' for 'prophetic anti-Judaism'; 'subordinating polemic' for 'Jewish-Christian anti-Judaism'; and 'abrogating anti-Judaism' for 'Gentilizing anti-Judaism'. See Smiga, *Pain and Polemic*, 12–23.

[46] E.g. William Paley used the verb in 1790 with respect to the Jewish law; *Horæ Paulinæ* (London: J. Davis for R. Faulder, 1790), 167. The 1876 English translation of F. C. Baur's book on Paul (*Paul: The Apostle of Jesus Christ* (London: Williams & Norgate, 1876), 1.59) speaks more generally of Judaism as having been 'superseded by Christianity'.

'supersessionism') has come to be used in a negative way, as a criticism of traditional Christian self-definition.[47]

This way of posing the question serves to shift the discussion from the external domain (Christian opinions, speech and action directed towards another group) to the internal (Christian self-definition and self-understanding). In some ways this is a more important question, since what Christians said and did with respect to Jews and Judaism was usually rooted in prior conceptions of how each of them related to scriptural Israel. This way of posing the question also helps to advance the discussion, especially where it has to do with written documents, since it draws attention to the intended function of the material. It makes a difference, for example, whether the Gospel of John is directed at an opponent with the aim of vilification and denigration, or whether its intended function is more internal, directed at a segment of the Christian community with the goal of creating and maintaining communal identity by drawing the lines between 'us' and 'them'. Distinctions in intended readership and rhetorical function are important.

Still, this set of terms has limitations. For one thing, it does not include some 'anti-Judaic' forms of Christian self-definition. To speak of supersession is to assume that at one time there was a positive value to Israel and its possessions, even if these have now passed entirely and without remainder to the Church. But some forms of the broader Christian movement saw very little value at all in the Israel of old. In the second century, for example, 'heretical' groups such as the followers of Marcion and the various groups that have come to be known as the Gnostics (after the Greek word for knowledge) believed that the Jewish people worshipped a different god, one who was inferior to the Father God revealed by Jesus. For such groups, the Israel of the past and the Jews of the present had been false, misguided or irrelevant from the beginning; the followers of Christ were distinct from and superior to Israel in categorical terms.

Further, and probably more importantly for our purposes, 'supersessionism' is used to lump together a variety of attitudes towards

[47] See e.g. the English version of Isaac's *Jesus and Israel*, 294; Baum's introduction to Ruether's *Faith and Fratricide*, 6, 21; and Franklin H. Littell, *The Crucifixion of the Jews* (New York: Harper & Row, 1975), 30.

scriptural Israel and contemporary Judaism that should be differentiated. Soulen has advanced the discussion somewhat by drawing a distinction between 'economic' and 'punitive supersessionism'.[48] The latter is the more negative category, in that Israel has been superseded precisely because of its sinfulness, clearly evident in the past but now culminating in the sin of rejecting Christ: 'Because the Jews obstinately reject God's action in Christ, God in turn angrily rejects and punishes the Jews', creating the Church to take their place.[49] Economic supersessionism, by contrast, is founded more on obsolescence than on sinfulness (though the two can be combined). Israel as an ethnic entity has had only a transient significance, in that its 'role in the economy of redemption is to prepare for salvation in its spiritual and universal form'. Thus '[e]verything that characterized the economy of salvation in its Israelite form becomes obsolete and is replaced by its ecclesial equivalent'.[50]

While this distinction is helpful, both categories tend to construct the relationship between the Church and Israel in disjunctive and discontinuous terms. In the one, Israel has been rejected; the Church replaces a failed people of God. In the other, Israel has been rendered obsolete; the Church replaces a people whose role and significance is a thing of the past. But in neither case is there any place for continuity between the two. These categories are perhaps applicable once Christianity has become fully separate from Judaism; in such a situation the idea that the 'new covenant' represents a fulfilment of the old would be indistinguishable from what Soulen calls economic supersessionism. In an earlier era, however, when Jewish believers made up the majority in the Church or, at least, when the Church contained identifiably Jewish and Gentile members and groups, 'fulfilment' was not simply a theological concept but was embodied

[48] R. Kendall Soulen, *The God of Israel and Christian Theology* (Minneapolis: Fortress Press, 1996), 29–33.

[49] Ibid., 30.

[50] Ibid., 29. Soulen also identifies a third category, 'structural supersessionism' (p. 31), having to do with the fact that the standard narrative that Christians constructed on the basis of Scripture moved from the fall of humankind in Adam to its redemption in Christ without assigning Israel any essential role in the story at all. In a sense, this has to do more with exclusion than with supersessionism per se. In such a canonical plot-line, Israel and its place in the biblical story of salvation is simply ignored, rather than seen as having being taken over by the Church.

in a group within the Church that also stood in social continuity with Judaism and the Israel of old. In this earlier era – which of course includes the New Testament writings – more attention needs to be paid to the various ways in which this element of continuity might have been understood and in which the inclusion of the Gentiles might have been conceived.[51]

The element of continuity is most readily apparent with respect to Jewish believers, especially those who continued to participate in the traditional structures of the Jewish world (Temple, Torah, etc.). Jewish Christians could readily have understood themselves as representing the remnant of Israel, the ones for whom the promises of messianic blessing were being fulfilled (e.g. Rom. 11.5), or even as representing the 'first fruits' of something that would include a greater portion of Israel in the future. In such a case, even if Israel is understood to have been reduced to a remnant, it has not been rejected and replaced by something else.

With respect to Gentiles, it is important to recognize that by including non-Jews in its fellowship the earliest Church was not necessarily turning away from its Jewish identity and behaving in un-Jewish ways. Judaism itself had already conceived of ways in which Gentiles might be brought into relationship with the God of Israel; several 'patterns of universalism' were already apparent within the Judaism of the period.[52] Judaism generally was ready to accept Gentiles as proselytes or converts, incorporating them fully within the people of Israel. Some Jews were prepared to accept the idea that Gentiles could relate in appropriate ways to the God of Israel without conversion, and thus be considered righteous as Gentiles. Many Jews expected that in the end-times, when, in fulfilment of the prophetic promises, God acted to redeem Israel, Gentiles would finally recognize the God of Israel and share in the end-time blessings. Early Jewish Christians could have conceived of incorporating Gentiles into their fellowship according to any of these patterns of thought. Indeed, as

[51] All that is needed for present purposes is to identify possible models of the relationship between Israel and the Church in the New Testament period; attempts to document the actual existence of this or that model in this period or to demonstrate its presence in this or that piece of primary literature can be taken up elsewhere.

[52] See Terence L. Donaldson, *Judaism and the Gentiles: Jewish Patterns of Universalism (to 135 CE)* (Waco, Tex.: Baylor University Press, 2007).

we will see when we turn to the New Testament directly, each of these patterns seems to have been present in the early Church, probably contributing to the documented disputes over the terms in which Gentile believers might be included (e.g. Acts 15). In all of these models the element of continuity between Israel and the Church is readily apparent.

Taking a step in the direction of discontinuity, another model for which there is some evidence is one in which Jewish believers are conceived of as the remnant of Israel but Gentiles are seen as having come in to replace the major portion of the Jewish people, who have been rejected by God because of their unbelief. While one can understand how this model could develop into Soulen's 'punitive supersessionism', the role assigned to a Jewish remnant sets it apart. Further, if Romans 11.26 looks forward to a future redemption for 'all Israel', so that the 'rejection' of the major portion of the Jewish people (11.15) is only a temporary thing, then in Paul's case the element of discontinuity is significantly softened.

Another step in this direction, though still preserving an element of continuity, is one in which Christ himself is seen as the ideal Israelite, the personification of Israel or the true remnant. Paul's argument that Christ is the real 'seed' of Abraham and heir of the promises made to him (Gal. 3.16) is one case in point. In this model those who believe in Christ come to share in his identity and thus, by extension, come to constitute a redefined Israel. The higher the proportion of Gentiles in the company of believers and the greater the degree of social separation from Judaism, of course, the more this model conforms to Soulen's 'economic supersessionism'.

Supersessionism, then, represents part of a broader set of models concerning the relationship between the Church and Israel. For it to be applicable to the New Testament, it would be necessary to show that the New Testament in whole or in part is to be located within this segment of the spectrum. Another way of putting it is to say that 'supersessionism' suggests a fixed and settled state of affairs, where one distinct entity supplants another. For this reason it is not a fully adequate category for analysing the elements of fluidity that are characteristic of at least many of the New Testament documents and the historical situation they reflect. The New Testament emerged out of, and was shaped by, a process of development and transition. A second-century author such as Justin Martyr may well be described as supersessionist, but he assumes that Christianity is essentially Gentile. The term would be much less applicable to the Jewish Christians that Justin knew in the middle of the second century and even less so to the earliest Jewish church in Jerusalem. Even when Gentiles come into the picture, there is a significant difference between the Gentile Christianity of Justin's day and a situation where Gentiles were thought of as having been incorporated into the messianic remnant of Israel.

Thus 'supersession' points us in the direction of important questions of self-definition, but it is a rather blunt instrument for differentiating the range of ways in which Christians defined themselves with respect to Israel and Judaism. Also, with its static-state assumptions, it is not entirely helpful for getting at the fluidity characteristic of the historical process that some have called 'the parting of the ways'. This, however, brings us finally to one other way in which the question has been posed.

Does the New Testament bear the marks of a painful 'parting of the ways'?

This question is a little different from the others; it has to do with broader issues that, while pertinent, can only be touched on here.

On the basis of the preceding discussion, it is apparent that the questions of interest to us need to be addressed within a historical framework that recognizes both diversity and development. As the terms are commonly used, 'Christianity' and 'Judaism' refer to social and religious phenomena that are themselves diverse. Perhaps it is going too far to speak of 'Christianities' and 'Judaisms', but the phenomena to which the plural forms seek to draw our attention are nevertheless real. On both sides, one characteristic of the diversity had to do precisely with the issues of self-definition vis-à-vis (the rest of) Judaism. In its original stage of existence, Christianity was one of several forms of Judaism engaged in a kind of sibling rivalry for the family inheritance. Further, what eventually can be described as Christianity and Judaism in their dominant forms are the result of a long and complex process by which two distinct religious movements emerged out of the common complex matrix of Second-Temple Judaism.

As we observed earlier, James Parkes referred to this process as 'the parting of the ways', and the term has gained wide currency.[53] It is useful for our purposes, since, as we have seen, the extent to which the New Testament writings might be described as antisemitic, anti-Judaic or supersessionist depends, in significant measure, on how this process is perceived and where in the process the individual writings are to be located. These descriptors might be appropriate with reference to a situation in which the ways have definitely parted; they are much less so when the ways are still intertwined and we are dealing with entities that are yet to become separate, distinct and well-defined.

Despite its usefulness, however, 'the parting of the ways' has come under critical scrutiny as a way of describing the process. In part, it is a question of timing and date: When was the process complete? At what point can it be said that the ways had parted in a final and definitive manner? Most commonly, scholars have pointed to the two Jewish revolts against Rome, with the Bar-Cochba rebellion of 132–5 CE completing a process of separation and self-definition that had begun with the earlier revolt of 66–73 CE.[54] As a variation of this approach, some scholars, recognizing that in some forms of Christianity (e.g. Paul's churches) the 'parting' was complete much earlier, prefer the plural form and thus speak of the 'partings of the ways'.[55] Recently, however, a number of scholars, pointing to evidence for continued interaction between Christians and Jews long after this date, have argued that 'the parting of the ways' attempts to tell 'a single and simple story of increased separation and isolation', when in reality the evidence speaks instead of 'a rich and variegated continuum of Jewish, Christian, and "Jewish-Christian" identities in dynamic competition, contact, and conflict',[56] continuing well into the Constantinian

[53] See e.g. the collection of papers edited by James D. G. Dunn, *Jews and Christians: The Parting of the Ways, A.D. 70 to 135* (Grand Rapids: Eerdmans, 1999).

[54] See e.g. the references to 135 CE in the subtitles of the volumes by Simon and Dunn cited above.

[55] E.g. James D. G. Dunn, *The Partings of the Ways Between Christianity and Judaism and Their Significance for the Character of Christianity* (London: SCM Press; Philadelphia: Trinity Press International, 1991).

[56] The quotations are taken from Adam H. Becker and Annette Yoshiko Reed (eds), *The Ways that Never Parted: Jews and Christians in Late Antiquity and the Early Middle Ages* (Minneapolis: Fortress Press, 2007), xi–xii, an important volume in this regard.

period and beyond. At the other extreme, Jossa has recently argued that the beliefs of the earliest Christians made this group quite distinct from Qumran or other Jewish sects, so that the Christian 'way' was set on a divergent path virtually from the outset.[57]

In addition to the question of timing, 'parting of the ways' has been criticized on conceptual grounds. For one thing, with the image of a single path diverging into two, the term suggests the assumption that Christianity and Judaism are two distinct, unitary and well-defined entities – an assumption that may serve the interests of orthodox and normative reconstructions of either group but only by minimizing the presence of diversity and deviation.[58] Boyarin takes this one step further, arguing that the even-handedness of the term treats Christianity and Judaism as analogous entities, two sub-species of the one species 'religion'. In his view this amounts to the imposition of a Christian category on Judaism, in that the difference between the two 'is not so much a difference between two religions as a difference between a religion [i.e. Christianity] and an entity that refuses to be one [i.e. Judaism]'.[59] For her part, Lieu has observed that far from being a neutral description, the term often functions as an ideological or theological construct.[60] While it may appear to provide an objective alternative to the subjective, partisan terms preferred by participants in the process (e.g. apostasy, heresy, blasphemy, rejection by God, and so on), often it seems to have been chosen more because it provides a positive framework for contemporary Christian–Jewish dialogue than because it necessarily offers an accurate description of the historical process.

Of course, none of this negates the main point that the New Testament needs to be understood and interpreted with reference to a historical process in which Christianity emerged from a Jewish matrix and developed into a distinct and separate entity. Still, there

---

57 Giorgio Jossa, *Jews or Christians? The Followers of Jesus in Search of Their Own Identity*, WUNT 1/202 (Tübingen: Mohr Siebeck, 2006).

58 E.g. see Becker and Reed, *The Ways That Never Parted*, 1–3, together with many of the essays in that volume.

59 Daniel Boyarin, *Border Lines: The Partition of Judaeo-Christianity* (Philadelphia: University of Pennsylvania Press, 2004), 8.

60 Judith Lieu, '"The Parting of the Ways": Theological Construct or Historical Reality?' *Journal for the Study of the New Testament* 56 (1994): 101–19.

have been significant differences in the way in which this process has been understood and reconstructed – differences closely connected to the identities and agendas of those doing the reconstruction – which means that even the terms in which it is described require critical scrutiny.

Setting directions

Thus there has been considerable diversity of opinion about the question of how Jews and Judaism are treated in the New Testament and even about the terms in which the question is to be posed. The primary purpose of this book is to describe and analyse this diversity rather than to evaluate the various viewpoints or to arbitrate the debates. So there is no more that need be said at this point about the substance of the question and the diverse responses that have been given. The previous pages, however, allow us to identify a number of variables or axes that will help us to describe and analyse the discussion of whether the New Testament (as a whole or in its individual parts) is antisemitic (or anti-Judaic or supersessionistic).[61]

One of these has to do with the self-understanding or self-definition that is present in the writing under examination. How does the author understand and construct the *identity of the group* to which he and his readers belong? What is its relationship with scriptural Israel? What is its relationship with contemporary Judaism? What is the relative status of Jewish and Gentile members within the group? Another concerns the *location of the author and intended readers* in the process of the 'separation' of 'Christianity' from 'Judaism' (the quotation marks are meant to signal the problems inherent in each of these terms). What degree of separation is reflected in the writing? A third has to do with the *rhetorical character of the text*. Each of the writings to be examined in the pages to follow was written with a specific and potentially identifiable set of purposes with respect to its intended readers. In each case, it will be important to consider such rhetorical characteristics as the following: the rhetorical function of an author's references to Jews or Judaism in the context of his

[61] These axes are related to the categories used above (subject, object, intent), though without corresponding to them exactly.

overall purposes in a particular rhetorical situation; the tone in which such references are made (e.g. whether statements are apologetical, polemical, pejorative or defamatory; whether there are explicit or implied value judgements; etc.); the legitimacy of the references to Jews or Judaism (i.e. the degree to which an impartial observer or even a Jewish reader would see the treatment as unfair, malicious, based on faulty information or skewed perceptions); and so on.

These axes – self-definition, degree of separation, rhetorical intent – will provide us with a three-dimensional grid that will help us to analyse and understand the diversity among New Testament interpreters. Where a given interpreter plots a New Testament text or writing on this grid will tend to determine the degree to which the interpreter sees the particular text as anti-Judaic (or antisemitic, or supersessionistic).

2

Matthew

> So when Pilate saw that he could do nothing, but rather that a riot was beginning, he took some water and washed his hands before the crowd, saying, 'I am innocent of this man's blood; see to it yourselves.' Then the people as a whole answered, 'His blood be on us and on our children!' (Matthew 27.24–25 NRSV)

In any discussion of anti-Judaism and the Gospel of Matthew, Matthew 27.25 stands squarely at the centre. The cry of 'the people as a whole' (*pas ho laos*) and its significance for the Gospel as a whole, however, has been variously interpreted. The variety of interpretation is conveniently illustrated in the work of Jules Isaac, Gregory Baum and Rosemary Ruether.

Isaac's main point has to do with the difference between the Gospels and their later Christian interpreters, who in his view imposed an anti-Judaic 'teaching of contempt' on the Gospels and thus misinterpreted the story of Jesus. The Gospels are not totally innocent, however. They are all tainted by a concern 'to reduce the responsibility of the Romans to a minimum in order to increase the responsibility of the Jews proportionately'; this taint appears in its most odious form in Matthew 27.25. While it is evident even from Matthew itself that the crucifixion was an act of the Roman governor encouraged by a 'caste' of Jewish leaders, the Gospel writer nevertheless declares that 'the Jewish people, whole and entire, took on themselves explicitly and expressly the responsibility for the innocent Blood'.[1]

Baum's response to Isaac centres on matters of context and intent. He argues that Matthew was written in the period after 70 CE when the Pharisees were establishing their dominance in post-war Judea and Matthew's own circle of Christians was still largely Jewish. Thus

[1] Jules Isaac, *Jesus and Israel* (New York: Holt, Rinehart & Winston, 1971), 295, 283, 334.

Matthew 'was the tragic witness of a schism in Israel, a dividing line running right through all sections of society, all provinces, all families, a schism between those who believed in Christ and those who did not'. Standing on one side of this schism, yet still within the larger Jewish world, Matthew saw himself and his community as the remnant of Israel, and thus as representing something anticipated by the prophets themselves. Further, like the prophets, Matthew's language of condemnation was uttered with the purpose not of vilification, but of moving Israel as a whole to repentance and conversion. While he had higher hopes for the common people than for the leaders – evident from the sharp contrast in the Gospel between the leaders and 'the crowds' – he nevertheless had not given up on the leaders themselves. Concerning Matthew 27.25, while Baum laments the harm that has been wrought through this verse by later interpreters, he feels that it is 'not . . . very significant in itself'. Although the crowds here are incited by their leaders to join in the call for Jesus' death, so that 'the whole people' assumes responsibility, Baum argues that this by no means amounts to national guilt and perpetual punishment, nor does it negate the fact that Matthew's language of condemnation is aimed at calling the people as a whole to repentance and conversion.[2] (We need to remember that Baum subsequently changed his opinion significantly. Statements about how Baum 'responds' or 'argues' refer to a way of thinking that he later repudiated.)

Ruether is also concerned with issues of context and intent, but in contrast to both Baum and Isaac she understands Matthew (along with Mark and Luke–Acts) to be fundamentally anti-Judaic. The attitude that comes to sharp expression in Matthew 27.25 is by no means a surface taint, but is part of a programme of self-definition that has been dyed into the fabric of Matthew from the beginning. The presentation of Jesus as the rejected, suffering yet vindicated Messiah, which finds its 'culmination' in 27.25, depends for its cogency on the parallel presentation of the Jewish leaders as the 'heirs

[2] Gregory Baum, *The Jews and the Gospel: A Re-Examination of the New Testament* (Westminster, Md.: Newman Press, 1961), 47, 66. Baum entertains, but rejects, the suggestion that since the formula 'X's blood is on the head of Y' often implies that X is innocent (e.g. Josh. 2.17–19; 2 Sam. 1.3–16; 3.29; 14.9; 1 Kings 2.29–33, 36–37; Jer. 51.35; Ezek. 18.10–20; 33.3–8), Matthew 27.25 represents a declaration of Jesus' innocence (pp. 69–70).

of the lineage of apostasy' going back to Israel's rejection, mistreatment and murder of the prophets sent to them by God. As in the case of Baum, context is important for Ruether; Matthew has to be read in the context of a bitter conflict with Pharisees in the situation after 70 CE. But in her view, a final separation from Judaism has already taken place. The Christians have been ejected from Judaism (e.g. 10.17) and have begun to find their place in the Gentile world (e.g. 28.18–20). For Matthew, the Jews as a whole are an apostate people (27.25); the Church is the sole heir of the promise.[3]

Quite clearly, the differences between Isaac, Baum and Ruether in their interpretation of Matthew 27.25 arise not simply from the passage in isolation but from more broad-based differences of opinion with respect to the meaning and purpose of the Gospel as a whole in its historical context. This, of course, is also the case with the scholarly interpretation of Matthew more generally, in which the range of viewpoints represented by these three authors is equally apparent. In the previous chapter I suggested that these interpretive differences can be considered along three axes: self-understanding or self-definition; degree of separation from Judaism; rhetorical function.

Self-definition in Matthew

How does the author[4] of Matthew's Gospel understand and construct the identity of the group to which he and his readers belong? The matter takes on a different complexion depending on whether we view the Gospel from its beginning or from its end, and the answer to the question will depend on what sense we make of the contrast between the two.

At the beginning of the narrative, the group that is to be the beneficiary of Jesus' ministry is clearly identified as the people of Israel. The genealogy with which the Gospel begins presents Jesus as the culmination of a line of descent from Abraham to the Messiah,

[3] Rosemary R. Ruether, *Faith and Fratricide: The Theological Roots of Anti-Semitism* (Minneapolis: Seabury, 1974), 64–95; the quoted word and phrase appear on pp. 94 and 72 respectively.

[4] For convenience we will refer to the author as Matthew, though without assuming anything about his actual identity.

which means that when he is introduced shortly afterward as the one who 'will save his people from their sins' (1.21), readers naturally understand 'his people' to be Israel, the family of Abraham. This is confirmed a few verses later when a passage of Scripture is applied to Jesus that speaks of 'a ruler who is to shepherd my [i.e. God's] people Israel' (2.6, based on Mic. 5.2). At the end of the Gospel, however, as the risen Jesus commissions the eleven disciples, his 'people' now seems to consist of a community of disciples drawn from 'all the nations' (*panta ta ethnē*; 28.19). Indeed, since *ethnē* often is used to refer to non-Jewish nations (or individuals), this verse may even suggest that the new community is not Jewish at all but is drawn from 'all the Gentiles'.

This contrast between beginning and end is part of a larger set of tensions within the Gospel as a whole. One of these has to do with the implied location of the author and his readers with respect to the world of Judaism. On the one hand, a number of things seem to suggest a location within the Jewish world. Some of these simply have to do with Jewish characteristics generally considered, such as the evident concern with the law of Moses (e.g. 5.17–20), or the assumption that Jewish terms or practices require no explanation (e.g. the phylacteries and fringes of 23.5; also compare 15.2 with Mark 7.2–4), or the description of Jerusalem as the 'holy city' (4.5; 27.53). Related to this is the tendency to treat Gentiles as outsiders and as inherently sinful or misguided; for example, on the topic of prayer, Jesus instructs his disciples not to 'heap up empty phrases as the Gentiles do' (6.7; also 5.47; 6.32; 18.17). Other statements go further by implying that the readers of the Gospel are fully within the Jewish world: they are subject to the scribes and the Pharisees because they 'sit on Moses' seat' (23.2–3); or they should pray that the time to flee Judea should not fall on the sabbath (24.20). On the other hand, however, a certain distance from the Jewish world seems to be suggested by the reference to 'their scribes' (7.29) or 'their synagogues' (4.23), and by the statement in 28.15 that the chief priests' version of the empty tomb story 'is still told among the Jews to this day'.

Another tension has to do with the scope of Jesus' ministry. On the one hand, in keeping with his task of 'sav[ing] his people from their sins' (1.21), Jesus restricts his own ministry (15.24) and that of his disciples (10.5–6) to 'the lost sheep of the house of Israel', in the latter case explicitly commanding his disciples not to go to the Gentiles or even the Samaritans. On the other, the Great Commission (28.19) is by no means the first time that Gentiles are placed into a positive relationship with Jesus. The first people to seek Jesus out (and worship him!) are the Gentile magi (2.1–12), and later both the centurion (8.5–13) and the Canaanite woman (15.21–28) are able to overcome any restrictions associated with their Gentile status and to benefit from Jesus' ministry (see also 4.15; 10.18; 12.21; 24.14).

Overlapping with the previous two points is a complicated collection of statements concerning Israel and the Jewish people. As has already been observed, the Gospel begins by identifying Israel as the people whom Jesus has come to save (1.21) and to shepherd (2.6), thus treating Israel as a whole in positive terms. A similar attitude is perhaps also present in Jesus' promise that the disciples would one day judge (or govern) 'the twelve tribes of Israel' (19.28).

Elsewhere, however, Matthew seems to be at pains to differentiate 'the crowds' (*hoi ochloi*) from the leaders. (While there is some variation in terminology – scribes, Pharisees, chief priests, elders, etc. – he seems to treat them as a single, undifferentiated group.) The crowds recognize the authority of Jesus' teaching, in pointed contrast to that of 'their scribes' (7.28–29); while the scribes accuse Jesus of blasphemy, the crowds 'glorified God, who had given such authority to human beings' (9.3, 8 NRSV); 'the crowds were amazed and said, "Never has anything like this been seen in Israel." But the Pharisees said, "By the ruler of the demons he casts out the demons"' (9.33–34 NRSV; also 12.22–24); the crowds shouted 'Hosanna', but the chief priests and scribes denounced him in anger (21.9, 15–16); the chief priests and the Pharisees perceived that Jesus was directing his parables against them, but they hesitated to arrest him because the crowds regarded him as a prophet (21.45–46); and the fierce denunciation of the scribes and the Pharisees in chapter 23 is carried out for the instruction and edification not only of the disciples but of the crowds as well (23.1). In addition, since the crowds are described as 'harassed and helpless, like sheep without a shepherd' (9.36), Matthew seems to imply that 'the lost sheep of the house of Israel' to whom Jesus was sent (10.5–6; 15.24) are to be identified with the crowds as distinct from the leaders (their false shepherds). Consistent with this is the way in which they respond to Jesus in the Gospel. They throng about him (4.23—5.1; 8.1; 9.36; 13.2; 14.13; 15.30; 19.2; 20.29); they are depicted as a ready harvest (9.37–38); they acclaim his mighty words (7.28–29) and works (9.8; 15.31); they acknowledge him as a prophet (21.11, 46) and even describe him in messianic terms (12.23; 21.9).

While the crowds are depicted as the beneficiaries of Jesus' ministry, the Jewish leaders are treated in unrelentingly negative terms from beginning to end. In addition to what we have already observed, we can note the following. They give Herod the information he needs for his attempt to kill the infant Jesus (2.4–6); they are denounced by John the Baptist as a 'brood of vipers' (3.7–10); Jesus picks up this term later, adding 'you are evil' for good measure (12.34); on three occasions he denounces them as 'blind guides' (15.14; 23.16, 24); he declares that the kingdom of God will be taken away from them (21.43), amplifying the point in three parables of rejection (21.28–32, 33–41; 22.1–14); and his denunciation of the Jewish leaders reaches a crescendo in chapter 23, with its series of harsh woes on the scribes and Pharisees.

This is not to say, however, that the depiction of the crowds is unrelentingly positive. Jesus' true family is to be found among the disciples, a group distinct from the crowds (12.46–50). Although the crowds may join with the disciples in forming the audience for three of Jesus' sermons, a distinction remains: in the Sermon on the Mount the disciples form an inner group (5.1), and in the other two Jesus withdraws from the crowds part way through to speak to the disciples alone (13.10; 24.1). In the Parables Discourse, Jesus says that the secrets of the kingdom of heaven have been given only to the disciples and not to the crowds (13.10–11). While the crowds as lost sheep may be the recipients of Jesus' ministry, the goal of his ministry is the creation of a 'church' consisting of disciples (16.18; 18.17; cf. 28.19–20).

Further, the crowds play a more negative role in the arrest and trial of Jesus. 'A great crowd' comes with Judas to arrest him (albeit 'from the chief priests and the elders of the people'; 26.47; also v. 55). Also, as we have seen, at the climax of the trial scene the crowds are 'persuaded' by the chief priests and elders to choose Barabbas over Jesus (27.20), and they join them in accepting responsibility for Jesus' death (27.25). Matthew describes this combined group of crowds and leaders as 'all the people' or 'the whole people' (27.25), perhaps implying that any distinction between crowds and leaders falls away at this point and that the Jewish people as a whole join in rejecting Jesus and taking responsibility for his death. If so, this negative depiction of Israel as a whole might be foreshadowed in Jesus' earlier declaration that the Gentile centurion exhibited a kind of faith that was not to be found 'in Israel' (8.10), and that 'many' like him would be present at the end-time banquet while the 'sons of the kingdom' were cast out (8.11–12).

Thus to pursue the questions that are of interest to us here we need to reckon with a complex set of tensions in Matthew's Gospel. A particular feature of the complexity is that both sides of the various tensions are present in material unique to Matthew and in the set of editorial changes that he has made to the sources commonly believed to have been at his disposal (Mark's Gospel and a collection of sayings (the Q source) also used by Luke). While this material will have a bearing on other matters to be discussed in the next two sections as well, here we are interested in the matter of identity and self-definition. How does Matthew perceive and construct the identity of the group to which his intended readers belong (or are being encouraged to belong)? In his view, what is the relationship between the Church (the community of disciples drawn from all the nations) and God's 'people Israel', as the latter would be understood by a reader of Micah 5.2 (cited in Matt. 2.6) and the rest of Israel's Scriptures? The degree to which Matthew can be described as antisemitic, anti-Judaic or supersessionistic depends on how one answers this question. Not surprisingly, there is a considerable range of opinion among interpreters.

Before turning to the range of opinion itself, it is appropriate to note that this state of affairs is the direct result of decisions that have to be made by any interpreter when faced with the kinds of varying details described above. The outcome of these decisions depends on one's understanding of what counts for evidence and what weight is to be given to different pieces of evidence. This depends in turn on the larger interpretive structure within which decisions are made. Such larger structures generally involve a set of tools used in well-defined ways (sometimes referred to as a methodology), together with the interpreter's own set of presuppositions, assumptions and commitments. While it lies beyond the scope of this book to engage in any extended or general discussion, we will nevertheless attempt to stay alert to the ways in which specific interpretive decisions are affected by such larger structures.

Rejection and replacement: two versions

One approach to the question of self-definition in Matthew is to understand the Gospel as a story of rejection and replacement: because of its rejection of Jesus, Israel has been rejected by God and has been replaced by a different entity, the Church. The first part of this story has to do with Israel's rejection of Jesus. In this reading of Matthew, such a plot line is hinted at already in the reaction of 'all Jerusalem' to the arrival of the magi (2.3); it is developed in the relentless opposition of the Jewish leaders to Jesus, beginning especially with chapter 12; it is reflected in Jesus' lament over Jerusalem for its treatment of the prophets and its unwillingness to respond to his appeal (23.37); and it culminates in the cry of 'all the people' (27.25), where any distinction between crowds and leaders is swallowed up in a corporate rejection of Jesus. The second part of the story is God's consequent rejection of Israel: 'the sons of the kingdom will be thrown into the outer darkness' (8.12); 'the kingdom of God will be taken from you' (21.43); Jerusalem's 'house will be left to you desolate' (23.38). The third, closely related, is God's choice of another people in Israel's place: just as the Gentile centurion exhibits a degree of faith not found 'in Israel', so 'many' like him 'will come from east and west' to share in the kingdom banquet (8.11–12); the kingdom of God, which has been taken from Israel, will be 'given to a nation that produces the fruits of the kingdom' (21.43). The whole story might be found in condensed form in Matthew's version of the parable of the great banquet (22.1–10): those who had been invited not only refused to come but even mistreated and killed those who brought them the invitation; in response, the king in anger 'sent his troops, destroyed those murderers and burned their city' (v. 7); then he invited other guests to replace those 'who were not worthy' (v. 8). The initial restriction of Jesus' mission to Israel simply serves to justify the final outcome of the story. God bent over backwards to give Israel every opportunity to respond; thus their rejection and replacement are fully justified.

This rejection–replacement reading of Matthew's Gospel is found in two forms. In the harder version, the Church is understood to be essentially Gentile; Jesus' command in the Great Commission that disciples be drawn from 'all the Gentiles' means that the Jews have been rejected in favour of the Gentiles. In the other version, perhaps the dominant one, the Church is seen to consist of Jews and Gentiles, but it is a new entity in which the Jews have no special ongoing status or significance; while the message is to be proclaimed to 'all the nations', Israel included, the Jews now represent simply one nation among many.

Israel rejected and replaced by a Gentile Church

For convenience, we will begin with the more extreme version. One of the earliest proponents of this reading of Matthew was Kenneth W. Clark, who described what he perceived to be 'the Gentile bias in Matthew'. Drawing attention to aspects of the Gospel that we have already observed, he came to the conclusion that 'the basic message of . . . Matthew' is 'the assurance that the Gentiles have displaced the Jews'.[5] Clark has been followed by many others. Douglas Hare, for example, building on an examination of the theme of persecution in Matthew, concludes:

> Henceforward the mission is not to Israel and the Gentiles but only to the Gentiles! The dual mission of Galatians 2:7–9 is replaced by the single mission of Matthew 28:19f.: 'Go, make disciples of all the Gentiles . . .'. These words form the climax of the gospel and express the considered opinion of its author.[6]

Lloyd Gaston provides another example. Endorsing Clark's conclusions about a Gentile bias, he states: 'More than any other Gospel, Matthew emphasizes the utter rejection of Israel . . . Israel rejected her Messiah; therefore God has rejected Israel.'[7]

What then about the more Jewish aspects of Matthew? There will be more to say on this in the next section, but for the present discussion this approach tends to understand the Gospel as a narrative that has to be read in light of its conclusion. Gaston describes

---

[5] Kenneth W. Clark, 'The Gentile Bias in Matthew', *Journal of Biblical Literature* 66 (1947): 165–72; here p. 172.

[6] Douglas R. A. Hare, *The Theme of Jewish Persecution of Christians in the Gospel According to St. Matthew*, Society for New Testament Studies Monograph Series 6 (Cambridge: Cambridge University Press, 1967), 148.

[7] Lloyd Gaston, 'The Messiah of Israel as Teacher of the Gentiles: The Setting of Matthew's Christology', *Interpretation* 29 (1975): 32; see also p. 33.

Matthew as 'a theological tragedy',[8] a term that anticipates more recent studies of the Gospels as narratives. Just as we cannot fully comprehend the plot of a novel until we get to the end and see the shape of what some literary scholars call the 'completed process of change' that the narrative describes, so we cannot understand the ambiguous place of Israel and the Jews in Matthew's story until we reach the end and see that the story culminates with the rejection of Israel and the calling of disciples from 'all the Gentiles' to take their place.

Essential to this reading of Matthew, then, is the decision that *panta ta ethnē* in 28.19 should be translated as 'all the Gentiles' rather than 'all the nations'.[9] To understand the choice between the two, a little background is necessary. In Greek, *ethnos* designates a 'nation' or (as the English derivative suggests) an 'ethnic group'. The translators of the Hebrew Scriptures into Greek chose *ethnos* (plural *ethnē*) as a rendering of the Hebrew *goy* (plural *goyim*). While *goy* in its singular form was occasionally used to refer to Israel (e.g. Gen. 12.2; Exod. 19.6; Isa. 51.4), the plural *goyim* refers almost exclusively to the other nations in contrast to Israel. The preferred term for Israel was *'am* (people), for which the Greek version generally uses *laos* (people). The two or three centuries prior to the time of Christ witnessed a further development in which *goyim* and *ethnē* came to be used not only of 'nations' but also of non-Jewish individuals. When we hear of three thousand *ethnē* (1 Macc. 5.22) or of the *ethnē* who lived in a particular town (2 Macc. 12.13) or of an Israelite selling animals to the *goyim* (*Damascus Document* XII 8–9), clearly we are to think of individuals rather than nations.

Returning to Matthew, there are many instances where *ethnē* clearly designates non-Jewish individuals or nations (especially 6.32; 10.5; 12.18, 21; 20.19). The question hinges on whether the addition of 'all' (*panta ta ethnē*) has an inclusive effect, so that the nation of Israel is included along with the others. The strongest argument against this and in favour of the exclusive rendering ('all the Gentiles') is that 28.19 seems to refer to individuals rather than to nations. Can nations be baptized or become disciples? The idea is not impossible perhaps, but it is certainly not the most natural reading. The

[8] Ibid., 27.

[9] For an argument in favour of this translation, see Douglas R. A. Hare and Daniel J. Harrington, '"Make Disciples of All the Gentiles" (Mt 28.19)', *Catholic Biblical Quarterly* 37 (1975): 359–69.

exclusive rendering might also find support in the contrast implied by 28.15: the false version of the empty tomb story has gained a hearing among 'the Jews', while the message of the risen Jesus is proclaimed to 'all the Gentiles'.

This reading, however, has not gone uncontested.[10] A good argument can be made that in the other occurrences of 'all the nations' in Matthew, Israel is included among them. In 25.32 'all the nations' are gathered in the presence of the Son of Man for the final judgement; it is hard to imagine that Israel would not be present. In 24.14, Jesus speaks of the gospel being proclaimed in the whole inhabited world (*oikoumenē*) and to 'all the nations'; just as Judea is part of the first, so the Jews must be part of the second. The issue is less clear in 24.9, where Jesus says that his disciples will be hated 'by all the nations because of my name'; still, he has just been speaking of persecution in synagogues (23.34), which suggests that Israel could be included among the nations. On the basis of such considerations, it can be argued that 'all the nations' is to be understood inclusively in 28.19 as well. Just as Israel is one of the nations to whom the message is to be proclaimed in Luke 24.47 ('to all nations, beginning from Jerusalem'), so it is to be counted among the nations from whom disciples are to be drawn (Matt. 28.19).

In support of this interpretation of 28.19, one might appeal to the Mission Discourse of chapter 10, where Matthew clearly expects the mission to Israel to last until the coming of the Son of Man (10.23). Thus 28.18–20 could readily be understood as representing an extension of the mission field (now to 'all the nations', not just to Israel) rather than the replacement of one field by another. This interpretation also allows for a smoother reading of the Jewish features of Matthew that were noted above, an aspect of the Gospel that is difficult to square with the idea of an exclusively Gentile outlook. Further, 28.15 need not be seen as a difficulty; just as Josephus (e.g. *Jewish War* 1.5) and Philo (*On the Virtues* 65) can speak of what goes on among 'the Jews' in the course of addressing a mixed audience of Jews and Gentiles, so in speaking of a story 'told among the Jews to this day' Matthew could simply be disclosing information that would

---

[10] See especially John P. Meier, 'Nations or Gentiles in Matthew 28.19?' *Catholic Biblical Quarterly* 39 (1977): 94–102.

not necessarily be common knowledge among the non-Jews in his intended audience.

Israel rejected and replaced by a Church drawn from the Jews and the Gentiles

This, then, leads to the softer version of the rejection–replacement approach to self-understanding in Matthew. In this version Israel is displaced from its special status as God's chosen nation and becomes a nation like the others, but the Jews still have an equal opportunity to become part of the new *ethnos* (cf. Matt. 21.43) that God is now gathering from among all the nations. Israel has been rejected and has been replaced in God's purposes by the Church, a 'third race'.[11] Nevertheless, Israel is still included among the nations from which the new community of disciples is drawn. In Meier's words:

> Israel, the unique chosen people of God, is indeed an entity of the past for Matthew; it had its hour of critical choice, and failed to choose rightly. . . . In Matthew's eyes they no longer enjoy the former privileged status of the chosen people of God (21.43). But they do qualify in Matthew's vocabulary as an *ethnos* (24.7). And so they do fall under the mandate of the risen Jesus to make disciples of *panta ta ethnē* (28.19).[12]

Is it really the case, however, that Matthew understands Israel to have been rejected categorically? As we have seen, the linchpin of this interpretation is the cry of 'all the people' in 27.25. But accepting responsibility for Jesus' death does not in itself imply that 'the people' were consequently rejected by God and that 'Israel' was emptied of its theological significance. Even if – as is quite likely – Matthew sees the destruction of Jerusalem as divine punishment on 'this generation' for its persecution of the line of prophets that culminates with Jesus (23.29–36), the idea of a definitive rejection does not necessarily follow. Josephus provides a near-contemporary example of a Jewish writer who saw the destruction of Jerusalem and the Temple as divine punishment (e.g. *Jewish War* 4.323), without seeing any negative

---

[11] For the term, see George M. Smiga, *Pain and Polemic: Anti-Judaism in the Gospels* (New York: Paulist Press, 1992), 83, though he prefers to speak of 'true Israel' (p. 91).

[12] Meier, 'Nations or Gentiles in Matthew 28.19?', 102.

consequences for the place and status of Israel. The idea that 27.25 seals the 'rejection of Israel' needs to be imported into the passage; it is by no means explicit. Indeed, since for Matthew Jesus' blood is 'poured out for many for the forgiveness of sins', in taking Jesus' blood on themselves 'all the people' in 27.25 are unwittingly identifying themselves with the precise means by which Jesus 'will save his people from their sins' (1.21). Rather than an indication of Israel's final rejection, perhaps 27.25 is meant to be another of the ironies that are common in the passion narrative.[13]

Further, it is worth noting that the supposedly rejected 'people' appear a little later in the narrative (27.64), in a scene where they once again 'are well disposed toward Jesus and open to being won over to him'.[14] The scene has to do with the request made to Pilate by 'the chief priests and the Pharisees', who are concerned that the disciples might steal the body and tell 'the people' that Jesus was raised from the dead, resulting in a 'last deception' that would be 'worse than the first'. Here 'the people' are differentiated from the Jewish leaders, which undercuts the idea that 'all the people' in 27.25 is meant to signify the nullifying of the distinction between the two that Matthew has been careful to make to this point. Further, the evident anxiety of the Jewish leaders depends on the assumption that 'the people' were readily susceptible to such a 'deception'. Matthew may well expect his readers to understand the scene ironically: despite the lengths to which the leaders were prepared to go (i.e. asking for a guard to be posted at the tomb), their efforts were to no avail, with the result that disciples were indeed able to 'tell the people' truthfully that Jesus had been raised, and the 'last deception' (i.e. the preaching of the gospel to the Jewish people) was indeed 'worse' than the first (i.e. the success of Jesus' ministry among the lost sheep of the house of Israel).

The Church as the lost sheep of Israel, joined by Gentiles

Thus it is possible to argue that the distinction between crowds and leaders is not erased by 27.25 and that Matthew remains fundamentally

---

[13] See Timothy B. Cargal, '"His Blood Be Upon Us and Upon Our Children": A Matthean Double Entendre?' *New Testament Studies* 37 (1991): 101–12.

[14] Anthony J. Saldarini, *Matthew's Christian-Jewish Community* (Chicago: University of Chicago Press, 1994), 29.

well-disposed to the 'lost sheep of the house of Israel' and hopeful that they will continue to respond in significant numbers to the 'testimony' of the disciples (10.18, 23) and to choose Jesus rather than the Jewish leaders as their rightful shepherd. On the basis of considerations such as these, a number of scholars argue that Matthew has an Israel-centred view of the group to which he and his readers belong.[15] In this interpretation of the Gospel, Matthew in his own setting continues to see Jesus primarily as the Messiah of Israel and to see his purpose as the restoration of Israel. For Matthew, the community of Jesus' disciples constitutes the remnant of Israel or the nucleus of a restored, messianic Israel. The current leaders of Israel, against whom Matthew's polemic is directed, are the false shepherds of the flock, the current manifestation of that portion of Israel that has always resisted and persecuted God's prophets. Such a self-understanding might be described as sectarian, the attitude of a minority group engaged in the process of defining itself over against a parent body (more on this in the next section).

It should be readily apparent that, if the theme of rejection in Matthew has to do with the leaders and those aligned with them and not with the people as a whole, much of the Gospel can be read as giving expression to such a remnant or sectarian outlook. In particular, this reading of Matthew can draw strength from those passages that treat Israel as an entity with ongoing significance: the end-time banquet as presided over by Israel's patriarchs, Abraham, Isaac and Jacob (8.11); the mission to the 'towns of Israel' as lasting until the coming of the Son of Man (10.23); the disciples as the ones who will serve as judges over 'the twelve tribes of Israel' (19.28); the expectation that a day will come when Jerusalem will say of Jesus, 'Blessed is he who comes in the name of the Lord' (23.39).

But what of the Gentiles? While one or two commentators have attempted to minimize the significance of the Gentiles for Matthew,[16] most are of the opinion that Matthew accepts a Gentile mission and

[15] J. Andrew Overman, *Matthew's Gospel and Formative Judaism: The Social World of the Matthean Community* (Minneapolis: Fortress Press, 1990); Saldarini, *Matthew's Christian-Jewish Community*; David C. Sim, *The Gospel of Matthew and Christian Judaism: The History and Social Setting of the Matthean Community* (Edinburgh: T&T Clark, 1998).

[16] See especially Sim, *The Gospel of Matthew and Christian Judaism*, 215–56.

includes those of non-Jewish origin in his intended readership. One approach would be to continue with a modified rejection–replacement reading, in which Gentiles come in to replace those unbelieving Jews who will be turned away from the end-time banquet (8.11–12). If this was Matthew's intent, however, it is surprising that it is absent from the passage in which the Gentile mission is initiated and clearly articulated for the first time. In 28.18–19 the basis for the Gentile mission is not the rejection of (part of) Israel but the vindication and exaltation of Jesus: 'All authority in heaven and on earth has been given to me. Go *therefore* (*oun*) and make disciples of all the nations.'

This leads to another approach, one in which Gentiles are seen as joining the restored portion of Israel rather than as replacing a rejected portion of Israel. This approach builds on the fact that Judaism in the first century was universalistic in its own way. Evidence from the later Second-Temple period indicates that Jews had developed several 'patterns of universalism', several ways in which Gentiles might be brought into a positive relationship with the God of Israel.[17] An openness to Gentiles need not imply a corresponding negative attitude to Jews and Judaism; what Clark depicted as Matthew's 'Gentile bias' may just as easily be seen as evidence of Matthew's Jewish character.

One of these patterns of universalism was proselytism – the incorporation of Gentiles through conversion as full and equal members of the people of Israel. This is the basis of Sim's view. Pointing to Matthew's strong emphasis on the law and to the absence of any distinction between Jew and Gentile in 28.18–20, he argues that a Gentile who wished to become a disciple was expected to become 'Jewish by conversion' and that 'membership of the people of Israel is an essential pre-requisite for the salvation offered by the death of the Christ on the cross'.[18]

But 28.18–20 says nothing about the law per se and Matthew seems to have little interest in those aspects of the law that would have differentiated Jew from Gentile (e.g. circumcision, food laws). This might suggest an approach in which it was thought that Gentiles could stand in a positive relationship to God without becoming proselytes. In one

[17] See Terence L. Donaldson, *Judaism and the Gentiles: Jewish Patterns of Universalism (to 135 CE)* (Waco, Tex.: Baylor University Press, 2007).

[18] Sim, *The Gospel of Matthew and Christian Judaism*, 247, 251.

such approach, Gentiles who worship the God of Israel exclusively and who live according to the law of Moses as it pertains to Gentiles are thought of as being acceptable to God and thus as righteous. Saldarini comes close to such a viewpoint when he speaks of Gentiles as attaining 'positive status by coming closer to Israel and Jesus and by affirming the law'.[19] Another approach is more eschatological in character – the expectation that when God fulfils the promises of salvation and redeems Israel, the Gentiles would have a share in the blessings of the end-times. The fact that the openness to the Gentiles in Matthew is possible only after the resurrection of the Messiah might provide a grounding for such an interpretation.[20]

Such approaches depend for their validity, however, on the idea of a Jewish remnant into which Gentile believers in Jesus might become incorporated (as proselytes) or with which they might become associated (as righteous Gentiles or eschatological guests). Is there enough evidence that Matthew sees the Jewish disciples of Jesus as constituting the remnant of Israel to support such an interpretation? Perhaps, though it might just as easily be said that for Matthew this role is played by Jesus himself. In the opening chapters of his Gospel, he seems to portray Jesus himself as Israel. Like Israel, Jesus was 'called out of Egypt' (2.15, quoting Hos. 11.1); like Israel he was tempted in the wilderness (forty days representing forty years; 4.1–11); he, rather than Jerusalem, is the one to whom the Gentiles bring their gifts of gold and frankincense (2.1–12; cf. Isa. 60.6); he is the one whose presence supersedes the Temple (12.6). It may be that for Matthew, Jesus has so taken over the role and identity of Israel that, as Gaston has argued, the primary form of continuity between Israel of the past and the Church of the present is provided by Jesus himself rather than by any Jewish-Christian entity.[21]

The Gospel then provides us with several possible answers to the question of self-identification, but without giving us clear guidance as to how to choose among them. Might we find further guidance by investigating the social location of Matthew and his intended readers?

---

19 Saldarini, *Matthew's Christian-Jewish Community*, 83.

20 See my *Jesus on the Mountain: A Study in Matthean Theology* (Sheffield: JSOT Press, 1985), especially ch. 11.

21 'The Messiah of Israel as Teacher of the Gentiles', 33.

Social location of Matthew and his intended readers

In the previous section we have been looking at the narrative itself, together with the world that it presents and invites its readers to enter. But what about the actual world of the author and his intended readers? What can be said about the world behind the text in contrast to the world within it? What can we know about the historical identity and situation of Matthew and his intended readers, especially with respect to the process of the separation of Christianity from Judaism? The cry of 'all the people' in 27.25 would take on one complexion if Matthew and his readers were part of a Gentile Church completely separate from the Jewish world, but quite another if they were part of a sectarian Jewish group within it.

We would be on surer ground here if we had independent information from sources other than the Gospel itself. Certainly there is an immense quantity of historical material that can help us in a secondary way. Jewish and Graeco-Roman sources allow us to construct a detailed history of Judea at least up to the end of the war with Rome (66–70 CE) and provide us with revealing glimpses into Jewish life in the diaspora. The vast array of Jewish literature from the Second-Temple period lets us know something about the various interests, concerns and preoccupations of the Jewish world. Rabbinic literature provides some insight into the emergence of the rabbinic movement in the aftermath of the destruction of Jerusalem. Archaeological discovery provides another window into Jewish social realities. Christian material provides us with substantial information pertaining to the first generation of the movement and then to its situation and history from the middle of the second century and beyond. Thus we are able to construct a picture, patchy in spots but nevertheless coherent, of the broader socio-religious world in which Matthew is to be placed.

But there is very little independent evidence (i.e. outside Matthew itself) concerning the origins and social location of Matthew's Gospel. There is a tradition, based on comments made by Papias, bishop of Hierapolis in the first quarter of the second century, that the Gospel was composed 'in the dialect of the Hebrews' (i.e. Aramaic) by Matthew, one of the Twelve. But while there is probably some historical core to the tradition, it cannot be taken at face value in either of its main assertions. The fact that the earliest references to

Matthew seem to appear in the letters of Ignatius (probably pre-117 CE), bishop of Antioch, has been used as evidence for Antioch as the place of origin of the Gospel, but the one certainly does not imply the other.

This means that our primary evidence for the social location of Matthew's Gospel has to come from the Gospel itself. Explicit evidence is scanty indeed. Matthew's version of the parable of the banquet (22.1–14) might suggest a date after the destruction of Jerusalem (note especially v. 7). The comment that Jesus' ministry in Galilee resulted in his fame spreading 'throughout all Syria' (4.24) suggests a frame of reference in which Syria is significant, but this does not necessarily imply an origin within Syria itself and thus is of little help in narrowing the search. In other words, anything that might be said about the real world behind the text will be the result of inferences drawn from the text of the Gospel itself.

The question of how to draw such inferences is a tricky one. Part of the difficulty has to do with method. In the heyday of redaction criticism (from the 1950s to the early 1980s), attempts to discern something about the life setting of the Gospels were made on the basis of the redactional (or editorial) tendencies of the evangelists. In the case of Matthew, for example, this involved an analysis of the editorial changes that Matthew made to his source material (Mark and Q); the resultant themes and emphases were then taken as indicators of the situation and concerns of the intended readers. This approach produced some definite results, though it was weakened somewhat by a tendency to assume that every detail in the text could be readily mapped onto a characteristic of the community, and a failure to differentiate clearly between the concerns of the evangelist and the situation of the intended readers. More recently, redaction critical insights have been refined with the aid of social-scientific analysis of group identity, boundary maintenance and sectarianism.[22]

Another approach to the Gospels in more recent time is narrative criticism, an analysis based on such narrative categories as plot, character, implied author, implied readers and so on. While some narrative critics have shied away from any discussion of the world

---

[22] See e.g. David L. Balch (ed.), *Social History of the Matthean Community: Cross-Disciplinary Approaches* (Minneapolis: Fortress Press, 1991).

behind the text, others have made use of some distinctive features of a narrative analysis. Important here is the general idea of the implied reader or audience – the profile of the reader or readers for whose benefit the story is being told – along with the identification of more specific points in the narration where the world of the story opens up into the world of its intended readers. In the case of Matthew, these points are found in the specific address to the reader in 24.15 ('let the reader understand'), statements about information being in circulation 'to this day' (27.8; 28.15) and references to those to whom the gospel would be proclaimed in the future (24.14; 28.19).

While a narrative approach is promising, it gets us into another difficulty, which stems from yet another tension within Matthew's Gospel. At some points in his telling of the story of Jesus, Matthew makes a clear distinction between circumstances that were pertinent in Jesus' own day and new circumstances that were present after his resurrection. The best example of this has to do with a mission to the Gentiles, which was prohibited during Jesus' own ministry (10.5–6; 15.24) but commanded after his resurrection. In contrast, there are points where the boundary between Jesus' earthly disciples and his later followers seems to have fallen away entirely. Chapter 10, for example, begins with Jesus' giving his disciples instructions for a short preaching mission in Galilee but shifts without warning at verse 16 into instructions for the Church living through difficult circumstances in the time leading up to 'the end' and the coming of the Son of Man (vv. 22–23). This tension between what some have called Matthew's 'historicization' on one hand and his creation of 'transparency' on the other makes it difficult to know what aspects of the Gospel might imply something about the circumstances of its intended readers and what aspects are meant to be part of a now transcended past.

The question of Matthew's social location, then, involves us necessarily with the various tensions that were explored in the previous section. Not surprisingly, the range of approaches that have been taken to the question overlaps considerably with the range of opinion described in the previous section and draws on much of the same material. Consequently, we can be brief.

At one end of the spectrum, as has been hinted at already, some have understood Matthew as having been written by a Gentile Christian for the benefit of a Gentile Church completely separate from Judaism. Of course, the Jewish characteristics of the Gospel cannot simply be ignored, but in this interpretation they are generally seen as a relic from the past. Matthew's community is seen as one that has undergone a dramatic transformation – from a Jewish sect admitting Gentiles to a completely Gentile Church looking back on a painful history of conflict with the synagogue. Jewish material has been retained in the Gospel partly in faithfulness to tradition and partly in service of the primary theme of the Gospel, namely, that God has rejected the Jews and turned instead to the Gentiles. Just as this understanding of Matthew's social location depends almost entirely on the evidence of 'Gentile bias' as discussed in the previous section, so the criticisms of this approach correspond to the arguments against such a bias. There is no need to repeat them here, but in addition questions can be asked about the plausibility of this approach. For one thing, would a strictly Gentile readership be able to perform the interpretive gymnastics that would be necessary to differentiate between Jewish elements in the Gospel belonging more properly to church archives, and material meant to guide and instruct the Church in the present? Further, can the heightened animosity directed towards the Jewish leaders really be understood as a reflection of social realities now belonging to the past?

The remaining approaches tend to locate Matthew in the situation within Judaism that emerged in the decades after the war with Rome (66–70 CE), when Jewish communities everywhere were having to deal with the loss of the Temple, the land and the Jewish state, and when – at least within Judea itself – the Pharisees were emerging as the dominant group. In such a context it would have been increasingly difficult for a deviant faction or sect to exist peaceably within the boundaries of Judaism, and the Pharisees, with their new centre of study in Jamnia, would have represented the source of the difficulty. Reference is often made in this connection to the *birkath ha-minim*, an addition to the Eighteen Benedictions of the daily synagogue liturgy that pronounced a curse against apostates and *minim* (deviants). While it is hard to know whether Christians were specifically targeted, the addition might provide some insight into the situation facing Jewish Christians in the latter part of the first century and beyond.

Among those who would locate the origins of Matthew's Gospel within this situation, however, there is vigorous debate over the precise location. Is Matthew's community still within the boundaries of Judaism, so that its debate with the scribes and Pharisees is *intra muros* (inside the walls)? Or has the rupture already occurred, so that the debate is *extra muros*? Once again the positions in this debate tend to correspond to those sketched out in the previous section. Those who understand self-definition in Matthew to be based on a rejection–replacement theme tend to see the intended readers of the Gospel as a mixed community of Jews and Gentiles now no longer within Jewish structures – a group separated from the synagogue, independent of its Jewish parent and attempting to forge its own distinctive identity as a community of believers in Jesus drawn from 'all the nations'.[23] Those who argue for a more Israel-centred approach, one that views the community of Jesus' disciples as the remnant of Israel (e.g. Sim, Saldarini), tend to see Matthew's community as a largely Jewish group with perhaps some Gentiles – a counter-cultural sect still within the boundaries of the Jewish world and attempting to present itself as the true representative of the people of Israel. Of course, these are not necessarily discrete alternatives, but probably need to be seen as points on a more complicated spectrum.

How we characterize Matthew's polemic will depend on where we locate the Matthean community on this spectrum or – to use a term introduced earlier – axis. But there is one further axis to be considered.

Rhetorical function of Matthew's treatment of Jews and Judaism

We have considered the content of Matthew's material dealing with Jews and Judaism (with special attention to the question of self-definition) and the social setting in which this content was shaped and to which it was directed. But what was its purpose? What was the intended function of this material with respect to its intended readers? And how did it accomplish this purpose? How did Matthew both draw on the substance of this material (what in classical rhetorical theory was called the *logos* of an argument) and invest it with emotional power (the *pathos* of an argument) to move his readers to adopt his intended conclusions, attitudes and courses of action?

---

[23] See e.g. Graham N. Stanton, *A Gospel for a New People: Studies in Matthew* (Louisville, Ky.: Westminster John Knox Press, 1993).

There is general agreement that the Gospel of Matthew – its polemical material included – is addressed to a Christian readership, broadly speaking. That is, it is addressed neither to Jews or a Jewish audience directly (in contrast, say, to some of Jesus' own statements), nor to those who stood outside both Judaism and the Christian movement (in contrast to a writing such as Justin's *Apology*, addressed, at least ostensibly, to the emperor). Further, it is widely believed that Matthew was written for a specific localized community (though this belief has recently been challenged[24]). In addition, there is general agreement that if Matthew is addressing a specific community, his purpose, at least in part, has to do with the specific needs or concerns of the community in its social context. Within this area of general agreement, a variety of more specific purposes have been suggested. Some see the Gospel as concerned primarily with teaching (cf. 28.19), suggesting that Matthew was intended as a catechetical document for disciples in-the-making or as an instruction manual for community leaders. Others have suggested that the Gospel addressed itself primarily to internal problems (attempting to reconcile the factions in a divided community, or to warn members against spiritual laxity). Still others see the community as facing threats from outside, so that the Gospel was written to fortify a community under persecution or to equip it for a struggle on two fronts – rabbinic Judaism on one side and antinomian (or law-rejecting) Christianity on the other.

But what of the anti-Jewish material in the Gospel (including the cry of 'all the people' in 27.25)? What was its intended function? And how did Matthew use it? Of course, answers to these questions will have a bearing on the more specific suggestions of purpose just mentioned, even as they will depend in turn on the range of positions described in the two previous sections. Here, however, we need to look at these questions more narrowly.

Several approaches can be identified. To be sure, none of them perceive Matthew to be interested in providing an accurate or even-handed description of Jewish leaders or Jewish concerns. Matthew is not a sympathetic or objective observer; his portrayal is decidedly

[24] See Richard Bauckham (ed.), *The Gospel for All Christians: Rethinking the Gospel Audiences* (Grand Rapids: Eerdmans, 1998).

negative. Still, the use to which he puts this negative portrayal can be variously construed.

One approach sees it as having to do with Jewish people directly. In this approach Matthew's primary intention was vilification. He wanted to lead his readers to share his negative attitudes towards the Jewish leaders, the Jewish people as a whole or Judaism more generally. As Isaac has put it, the Gospel writers were engaged in a '[r]eal competition to see who will make the Jews more odious', and the prize went to the author of Matthew 27.25. Later readers who saw in this verse justification for their 'frenzies and crimes' were simply expressing in action the attitudes that the text intended to inculcate in its readers.[25]

A second type of approach, perhaps the most widely represented, understands Matthew's negative depiction of Jews and Judaism as directed inward, with the goal of social formation. Whether the community addressed in the Gospel is understood as a Jewish sect, a mixed group engaged in the process of constructing a separate identity or a completely separate Gentile community, the negative depiction of 'the other' contributed to the process of marking out the boundary between 'us' and 'them', and of shaping the identity and self-perception of those inside the boundary. Such a use of negative stereotypes is common in most cultural situations, and Johnson has argued, on the basis of a survey of inter-group polemic in Graeco-Roman antiquity, 'that the way the NT talks about Jews is just about the way all opponents talked about each other back then'.[26] Anti-Jewish polemic is to be seen not as an attempt to describe the characteristics of actual Jewish neighbours nor as something intended primarily to inculcate negative attitudes towards 'the other', but as a means of reinforcing a sense of group identity and solidarity among the members.

A variation of this approach is one which emphasizes the distinction between the Jewish leaders and the crowds. The polemical characterization of the Jewish leaders is designed not only for purposes of self-identification but also to encourage the common

[25] Isaac, *Jesus and Israel*, 338, 240 respectively.

[26] Luke Timothy Johnson, 'The New Testament's Anti-Jewish Slander and the Conventions of Ancient Polemic', *Journal of Biblical Literature* 108 (1989): 429.

Jewish people – the 'lost sheep of the house of Israel' – to accept this identity for themselves and to join the group.

Taking this one step further, some have taken the position that Matthew's anti-Jewish polemic functions as a means not only of recruitment and social formation but also of self-criticism. In his study of chapter 23, for example, Garland argues that Matthew's primary aim in this harsh denunciation of the scribes and Pharisees is to warn his own community, especially its leaders, about negative characteristics and behaviour to which they too were susceptible. Even though Jesus here addresses the Jewish leaders directly ('woe to you!'), the actual audience of the discourse is the crowds and his disciples (v. 1). Further, in vv. 8–12 Matthew depicts Jesus as turning from the Jewish leaders to the crowds and disciples, to warn them about precisely the same behaviour. The fact that Jesus himself is elsewhere depicted as the positive counterpart to such negative behaviour (compare vv. 11–12 with 20.26–28) underscores the argument that 'the condemnation of the scribes and Pharisees is utilized more as a teaching opportunity for the benefit of the disciples'.[27]

Matthew's rhetorical intentions, then, can be variously assessed, with a corresponding variety in the way in which we might assess his treatment of Jews and Judaism.

Concluding observations

Is Matthew antisemitic? anti-Judaic? supersessionistic? How we answer these questions will depend on where we locate Matthew's Gospel with respect to the three axes discussed above – self-definition, social location and rhetorical function. If we choose coordinates at one extreme – deciding (1) that Matthew understands the Church as a Gentile entity, whose existence is predicated on the rejection of the Jews as the people of God (self-definition); (2) that the Gospel was written in and for a Gentile Church now totally separated from the world of Judaism and existing in a hostile relationship with it (social location); and (3) that the intended purpose of its polemic was to

---

[27] David E. Garland, *The Intention of Matthew 23*, Supplements to Novum Testamentum 52 (Leiden: Brill, 1979), 122.

vilify the Jews as a whole and to inculcate anti-Jewish attitudes in its readers – then Matthew's Gospel is certainly supersessionistic and anti-Judaic, and might be at least latently antisemitic. If instead we locate the Gospel at the other extreme – deciding (1) that Matthew understands the Church to be the messianic remnant of Israel; (2) that the Gospel was written in and for a Jewish sect or renewal group still existing within the world of Judaism and participating in its structures and institutions, even if standing in critical opposition to the current Jewish leadership; and (3) that the polemic was directed solely against the Jewish leaders with the aim of encouraging the rest of the Jewish people to choose Jesus as their teacher and leader instead – then the Gospel is neither antisemitic nor anti-Judaic and may not even be supersessionistic.

The three axes are not completely independent; decisions about where to locate the Gospel on one axis will limit the options for the other two. If Matthew understands the Church to be a Gentile entity, for example, he could not have been writing in and for a community of Jewish believers existing within the world of Judaism. Still, there are a number of possible sets of coordinates in between these two extremes, and thus a number of possible answers to the questions. Which of the possible answers we take to be most plausible depends on the decisions we make as interpreters about the issues represented by each of the axes.

3

Luke–Acts

> Let it be known to you then that this salvation of God has been sent to the Gentiles; they will listen. (Acts 28.28 NRSV)

On three occasions in the Acts of the Apostles, Luke depicts Paul as declaring to a Jewish audience that, because of their rejection of his message, he is turning to the Gentiles (Acts 13.44–48; 18.5–7; 28.25–28). This depiction is striking not only for its repetition but also because the third instance is also the conclusion of the narrative. This raises the possibility that Luke–Acts as a whole can be read as a story of the definitive rejection by the Jews of both Jesus and the gospel, and their replacement in God's purposes by the Gentile Church. Once again we will allow Jules Isaac, Gregory Baum and Rosemary Ruether to introduce us to the issues and to the range of interpretive options.

In keeping with his concern to demonstrate the contrast between the (Jewish) story of Jesus and the (anti-Jewish) interpretation of this story by the later Church, Isaac is quick to point out examples of Luke's positive attitude towards Jews and Judaism. He notes, for example, the emphasis in Luke's first two chapters on the Jewishness of Jesus and the simple Jewish piety of his parents, paying particular attention to the 'specifically Israelite' themes contained in the Magnificat (Luke 1.46–55).[1] He also comments on the 'very different tone' that pervades Luke's account of the healing of the centurion's slave (Luke 7.1–10), in contrast to sharp Israel–Gentile polarity in Matthew (8.5–13).[2] He also points to Luke 19.48 ('all the people were spellbound by what they heard'), expressing the wish that later interpreters had paid more attention to this occurrence of 'all the people'

[1] Jules Isaac, *Jesus and Israel* (New York: Holt, Rinehart & Winston, 1971), 17.
[2] Ibid., 191–3.

than to that in Matthew 27.25.[3] While he does not give much focused attention to Acts (he is concerned primarily with Jesus and the Gospels), he does note both Peter's statement to the 'Israelites' of Jerusalem that their part in Jesus' death was due to ignorance and thus could be remedied by repentance (Acts 3.12, 17), and Luke's emphasis on the considerable success of the mission to the Jews in Jerusalem and Judea.[4] At the same time, however, Isaac sees Luke as equally implicated in the competition to shift responsibility for Jesus' death from the Romans to the Jews. While he awards the prize in this dubious competition to Matthew (for 27.25), he observes that in Luke Pilate pronounces Jesus' innocence no fewer than three times (23.14–16, 20, 22) and that the rejection of Pilate's offer (to release Jesus) by the 'the chief priests, the leaders and the people' does not fall far short of Matthew.[5] Further, with respect to Acts, it is easy to see how Isaac might have implicated Luke in the development of such themes as the culpability of the Jewish people as a whole, God's rejection of the Jews and the subsequent turning to the Gentiles.

The way in which Isaac might have read Acts in an anti-Judaic way is clearly apparent from Baum's work. Baum is prepared to recognize a link between Jewish rejection of the gospel and the mission to the Gentiles in Paul's three declarations (Acts 13.44–48; 18.5–7; 28.25–28). He minimizes the significance of this, however, by making a distinction between the land of Israel and the diaspora. In the land of Israel, the ministry of Jesus and the preaching of the apostles does not meet with rejection but instead produces a schism within Israel. While this schism has to do with the significance of Jesus, it also corresponds to a distinction, deliberately drawn by Luke, between the proud and self-righteous on one hand and the humble and repentant on the other. The followers of Jesus and the members of the earliest Church, drawn from the latter, are 'the true representatives of Israel'.[6] When Gentile believers appear in the narrative, Luke understands them as having been added to this remnant of believing Jews ('a renewed

---

3 Ibid., 348.

4 Ibid., 361, 239, 387.

5 Ibid., 337, 326.

6 Gregory Baum, *The Jews and the Gospel: A Re-Examination of the New Testament* (Westminster, Md.: Newman Press, 1961), 77.

Israel') in keeping with 'the universalistic ideal of the prophets'[7] rather than as having been chosen by God to replace the Jews. It is only in the diaspora that we find the mission to the Gentiles being justified on the basis of a lack of Jewish response, and even here the preaching of the gospel to Jewish audiences produces a schism. In Baum's view, Luke envisaged a Church in two branches – a Jewish Church in the land of Israel, 'attached to the Law as its national heritage', existing alongside a Church 'in the pagan world destined for the Gentile populations'.[8] Further, even though Israel no longer stands at the centre of God's dealings with the world but exists 'side by side with other nations' in the Church, Baum believes that Luke continues to see Jesus as the redeemer of Israel, through whom 'the future salvation of the unbelieving section of Israel' remains assured.[9]

For Ruether, such a claim about the significance of Jesus for Israel is itself inherently anti-Judaic, in that it leads directly to a christocentric interpretation of Israel's Scripture that, on its negative side, involves a repudiation of Israel's own scriptural self-understanding. In addition, she sees Paul's declaration to the Jews in Rome (Acts 28.25–28) simply as a culmination of a theme that has dominated Luke's purposes from the outset. Right from the beginning of his narrative, from Simeon's recognition of Jesus as 'a light for revelation to the Gentiles' (Luke 2.32) and the rejection that Jesus experienced in Nazareth (4.16–30), Luke's storyline has been governed by the 'dogmatic theme' that 'the rejection of the gospel by the "Jews" and their constant efforts to "kill" God's messengers result in the turn from the mission to the Jews to that of the Gentiles'.[10]

The work of Isaac, Baum and Ruether serves to indicate the range of options that might be taken by interpreters of Luke–Acts. Once again we will explore the interpretive options along three axes, beginning with the topic of self-understanding or self-definition.

---

[7] Ibid., 153.
[8] Ibid., 165.
[9] Ibid., 166.
[10] Rosemary R. Ruether, *Faith and Fratricide: The Theological Roots of Anti-Semitism* (Minneapolis: Seabury, 1974), 89.

Self-definition in Luke–Acts

While Luke–Acts is similar to Matthew in a number of respects, there are important differences that will have a bearing on our discussion. For one thing, Luke has supplemented his Gospel with a second volume, dealing with the life of the early Church. While Matthew's attitudes towards the post-resurrection period have been overlaid onto his account of Jesus' mission and thus usually are implicit at best, Luke devotes half of his two-part sequential account to the early Church. Further, the emergence of Gentile Christianity from its Jewish origins is clearly a central concern for Luke, evident both in the details of the narrative and in its overall geographical and geo-religious arc as it moves progressively outwards from Jerusalem to Rome. One consequence of this geographical movement is that Luke deals directly with diaspora Judaism, displaying a particular interest in Gentiles who already stand in some sort of relationship with the Jewish community – both proselytes (Acts 2.10; 6.5; 13.43) and those sympathizers whom he describes as 'God-fearers' (10.2, 22; 13.16, 26) or 'worshippers of God' (16.14; 17.4, 17; 18.7). In addition, despite a certain tendency to smooth over any evidence of conflict and disagreement, Luke is nevertheless aware that the movement into the Gentile world had its share of both. Also, he seems to make a clear distinction between Jewish and Gentile 'Christians' (a term that he uses with reference to both Jewish and Gentile believers; Acts 11.26). While Gentile Christians are bound only by the terms of the 'apostolic decree' (Acts 15.19–21), Luke seems to take it for granted that Jewish Christians will continue to 'observe and guard the law' (Acts 21.24), even to the point of being 'zealots for the law' (Acts 21.20). Finally, in contrast to Matthew, where debate and conflict with the synagogue is simply a two-sided affair, a third party is frequently in view in Luke–Acts, as Roman officials are regularly called on to adjudicate disputes between the two, and who, just as regularly, pronounce in favour of the Christians. Luke seems to attach considerable importance to the opinion of the wider Roman world towards the emergence of Gentile Christianity and its relationship to its Jewish origins.

Nevertheless, Luke–Acts is similar to Matthew in that it presents us with a striking – and puzzling – contrast between its beginning and end. The story of Jesus' birth in the opening chapters of Luke (chs 1—2) is populated almost entirely by pious Israelites who are quietly waiting for the promised end-time redemption of Israel and who both hear and proclaim the message that this long-awaited salvation is about to be accomplished through John and Jesus.

Luke repeatedly emphasizes the righteousness and Torah-piety of these people. Zechariah and Elizabeth were both 'righteous before God, living blamelessly according to all the commandments and regulations of the Lord' (1.6). When John is born, they circumcise him on the eighth day (1.59), as was required by the Torah (Lev. 12.3). Jesus too is circumcised on the eighth day (2.21), after which Mary and Joseph carry out the rite of purification at the Temple 'according to the law of Moses' (2.22–24), not leaving until 'they had finished everything required by the law of the Lord' (2.39). At the Temple they encounter Simeon, who was 'righteous and devout' (2.25), and Anna, who 'never left the Temple but worshipped there with fasting and prayer night and day' (2.37).

In addition, Luke presents these people as united in their hope for eschatological redemption, a redemption depicted in traditional Jewish terms. Simeon was looking for 'the consolation of Israel' (2.25), Anna for 'the redemption of Jerusalem' (2.38). Mary, informed by the angel Gabriel that her son would sit on 'the throne of his ancestor David' (1.32), later declares that through her God was 'help[ing] his servant Israel, . . . according to the promise he made to our ancestors, to Abraham and to his descendants for ever' (1.54–55 NRSV). Zechariah, after finally regaining his voice, rejoices that God has acted to redeem 'his people' Israel by 'raising up a horn of salvation for us in the house of his servant David', thus 'remember[ing] his holy covenant' (1.68–69, 72). Since in all of this Jesus (along with John) is declared, first by angels (1.32–33; 2.11) and then by others (1.69–73; 2.27–32, 38), to be the one to accomplish this salvation, the opening chapters of Luke create clear expectations that the story to follow will have to do with the fulfilment of the hope of messianic salvation that faithful Israelites had nourished since the time of the prophets. Gentiles are mentioned once, in Simeon's hymn of praise (2.32). While the reference is positive (the salvation to be accomplished through Jesus will serve as 'a light for revelation to the Gentiles'), the expectation seems to be that any positive benefit for the Gentiles will exist alongside and in conjunction with 'the glory of [God's] people Israel'.

By the time we reach the end of Acts, however, a story that had begun in the Jerusalem temple (Luke 1.8–9) comes to its end in the capital city of the Gentile world, as Paul, the missionary to the Gentiles par excellence and now a Roman prisoner, proclaims the message to 'all who came to him' (Acts 28.30–31), thus fulfilling his ambition of extending the mission as far as Rome (Acts 19.21). Here Luke seems to present quite a different rationale for the salvation of the Gentiles. Acts 28.23–28 recounts Paul's meeting with the Jewish community in Rome. After a whole day spent 'trying to convince them about Jesus both from the law of Moses and from the prophets' (28.23), he concluded the session by quoting Isaiah's denunciation of a people incapable of seeing and hearing (Isa. 6.9–10), and then saying: 'Let it be known to you then that this salvation of God has been sent to the Gentiles; they will listen' (Acts 28.28). Simeon had envisaged a 'salvation [of God]' that would encompass both Israel and the Gentiles (Luke 2.30); Paul's declaration seems to imply that the beneficiaries of 'this salvation of God' are now the Gentiles instead of Israel. Since readers might have expected some other conclusion to the narrative – Paul's trial, for example, or further interaction with the Roman believers (Acts 28.15) – Luke's choice to end the narrative this way gives added force to such an implication.

As with Matthew, then, our reading of Luke–Acts will depend on the sense we make of the contrast between the expectations aroused at the (very Jewish) beginning of the narrative and the quite different state of affairs that we arrive at when we get to the (emphatically Gentile) end. Scholarly interpretation of Luke–Acts can be differentiated according to whether and to what extent the expectations raised in the beginning of the narrative are fulfilled at the end.

Expectations fail: Israel rejected and replaced by Church

In one very common reading of Luke–Acts, any expectations concerning the messianic redemption of Israel that might have been raised in the first two chapters turn out in the end to have failed. The message of salvation proclaimed to Israel first by Jesus and then by the apostles is systematically rejected, with the result that Israel in turn is rejected and 'this salvation of God' is sent to the Gentiles instead (Acts 28.28).

For those who read Luke–Acts in this way[11] the overall intention of the work is determined by its ending. Some of the evidence in support of this reading has already been observed: the effect of the ending, especially when other endings might have been anticipated; the repetition of the phrase 'the salvation [of God]' (cf. Luke 2.30; Acts 13.26), but this time with exclusive reference to 'the Gentiles' (Acts 28.28); the fact that this turning to the Gentiles is the third in a sequence. In addition, attention is drawn to the shift from a local situation, one involving just the leaders of the Jewish community in Rome (28.17, 23), to a general conclusion concerning Israel as a whole. Since 'this people' (28.26) is set in contrast with 'the Gentiles' (28.28), it is clear that Luke intends Paul's quotation of Isaiah's denunciation to apply not simply to Roman Jews but to Israel itself. While a similar shift from the local to the categorical is found in the other two related passages ('the Jews' (13.45; 18.5) . . . 'the Gentiles' (13.46, 47; 18.6)), the final passage differs in that it contains no explicit Jewish opposition to Paul. Even though 'no opposition arises', 'Paul turns viciously on his auditors, sounding very much like Stephen in quoting Isa. 6.9–10 against them',[12] the unprovoked nature of the denunciation thus providing a clear indication of Luke's beliefs and intentions.

As is suggested by Sanders' reference to Stephen, there is no shortage of material earlier in Luke–Acts that might serve to lead up to and reinforce the ending. Sanders draws attention to the parallels between the speech with which Acts ends and that with which Jesus' ministry begins. Jesus' inaugural sermon in the Nazareth synagogue also contains a citation from Isaiah and an unprovoked denunciation of Israel. Despite the fact that 'all spoke well of him' for his reading

---

[11] As noted already, this approach is taken by Rosemary Ruether. See also Ernst Haenchen, *The Acts of the Apostles: A Commentary* (Oxford: Blackwell, 1971), 415–18, 539–40, 729–32; Jack T. Sanders, *The Jews in Luke–Acts* (Philadelphia: Fortress Press, 1987) and 'The Jews in Luke–Acts', in *Luke–Acts and the Jewish People*, ed. Joseph B. Tyson (Minneapolis: Augsburg, 1988), 51–75; George M. Smiga, *Pain and Polemic: Anti-Judaism in the Gospels* (New York: Paulist Press, 1992), 133; Lloyd Gaston, 'Anti-Judaism and the Passion Narrative in Luke and Acts', in *Anti-Judaism in Early Christianity*, vol. 1: *Paul and the Gospels*, ed. Peter Richardson with David Granskou (Waterloo, Ont.: Wilfrid Laurier University Press, 1986), 127–53.

[12] Sanders, 'The Jews in Luke–Acts', 72.

of Isaiah (Luke 4.22), Jesus quickly turns on them, denounces them for failing to accept him as a prophet, and pointedly makes reference to Gentiles who were the beneficiaries of Elijah's and Elisha's ministry, even though there were many widows or lepers in Israel at the time (4.24–27). What has happened to the humble, pious Israelites of chapters 1 and 2? The tone of Jesus' inaugural sermon might seem to send a clear signal that the earlier expectations are not to be realized. Indeed, looking back at these chapters from the perspective of chapter 4, several clouds appear already on Luke's optimistic horizon. Zechariah's initial response to Gabriel's message (1.18–20) is one of unbelief, which is met by rebuke and punishment (albeit temporary). Despite Simeon's exultation over God's salvation, he also observes that Jesus will be 'opposed' and will bring about 'the falling and rising of many in Israel' (2.34). The precedence given to the 'falling' over the 'rising' might seem to strike an ominous note, as might also be the case with the precedence he gives to the 'light for revelation to the Gentiles' over the 'glory to your people Israel' (2.32).

Further, those who read Luke–Acts in this way are not at all embarrassed by the positive tone of the first two chapters. In fact, this can readily be seen as part of a wider theme in Luke–Acts, one that emphasizes the fidelity of both Jesus and the Church to the traditions of Israel. In the account of Jesus' trial, for example, Luke goes out of his way to present Jesus as innocent of any violation of Judaism. Absent from his account are the charges of threatening the temple (Mark 14.57–59) or of blasphemy (Mark 14.64). The only charge brought against him is that of claiming to be the 'king of the Jews' and stirring up the people (Luke 23.3–5). His innocence is attested to by Pilate (23.4, 14), Herod (23.15), the Roman centurion at the cross (23.47) and even one of the criminals crucified with him (23.41). The earliest Church, likewise, is presented as remaining faithful to the institutions and aspirations of Judaism. They celebrate Pentecost (Acts 2.1) and gather in the Temple (2.46; 3.1; 5.42). They continue to look for the sending of Israel's appointed Messiah (3.20) and the consequent restoration of 'the kingdom to Israel' (1.6; also 3.21). Even Paul is presented as a Jew who frequents the synagogue (13.14; 14.1; 17.1, 10; 18.4, 19; 19.8), offers sacrifice at the Temple (24.11, 17) and observes Jewish traditions (16.3; 18.18; 21.24). While some Jerusalem Christians believe that he teaches diaspora Jews to forsake the law of Moses, Luke presents him as innocent of the charge

(21.21–24). Luke's point, then, is 'that Jesus and the church did not turn their backs on the Jews; it was the other way round'.[13]

This point (so it is argued) becomes abundantly clear in Acts. Even in the early preaching by the apostles in Jerusalem, while Peter recognizes Jewish culpability for Jesus' death (2.23; 3.13–15; 4.10, 27; 5.28–30), he is willing to excuse it on the grounds of 'ignorance' (3.17) and to extend another opportunity for repentance (2.38; 3.19; 5.31). Yet opposition increases, so that by the time we get to Stephen's speech, any call to repentance has fallen away as Stephen aligns Jewish opposition in the present with all those who persecuted the prophets and resisted the Holy Spirit in the past, whom he describes both as 'your ancestors' and as 'those who received the law' (7.51–53), the latter designation virtually extending the denunciation to the whole of Israel. From here on, the story is increasingly one of Gentile belief and Jewish opposition. Even though Paul consistently begins his preaching in the synagogue (13.14; 14.1; 17.1, 10; 18.4, 19; 19.8), his preaching just as consistently provokes opposition by 'the Jews' (13.45; 14.4; 17.5; 18.5–6, 12; 20.3, 19). Thus by the time we read Paul's final denunciation of 'this people', it is clear (says Haenchen) that Luke 'has written the Jews off' in favour of the Gentiles.[14]

Of course, not all are written off. The apostles are all Jews, as are the members of the Jerusalem church ('many thousands'; 21.20). Even in the diaspora, some of Paul's Jewish hearers respond positively and believe (13.43; 17.4, 11–12; 18.8). Most scholars who agree with Haenchen would make a distinction 'between the collective response of Jews as a whole and the response of individual Jews'.[15] Although some Jews do believe, 'the Jews' as a collective entity do not, and by the end of Acts it is clear that the future belongs to the Gentiles. This, says Gaston, 'is what makes Luke–Acts in its final form and as a totality anti-Judaic'.[16] Sanders takes this one step further. Noting that opposition to Paul from Jerusalem believers increases through the

[13] Sanders, *The Jews in Luke–Acts*, 161.

[14] Ernst Haenchen, 'The Book of Acts as Source Material for the History of Early Christianity', in *Studies in Luke–Acts*, ed. Leander E. Keck and J. Louis Martyn (Minneapolis: Augsburg, 1966), 278.

[15] Joseph B. Tyson, 'The Problem of Jewish Rejection in Acts', in *Luke–Acts and the Jewish People*, ed. Joseph B. Tyson (Minneapolis: Augsburg, 1988), 126.

[16] Gaston, 'Anti-Judaism and the Passion Narrative in Luke and Acts', 139.

narrative – from the 'some' of Acts 15.1 and 5 to the 'many thousands' of 21.20 – he takes the position that for Luke the Jerusalem Christians, 'like their non-Christian kin, prefer following Moses to repenting and believing in true contrition,'[17] and thus come to share in Luke's blanket condemnation of 'the Jews'. He concludes with this harsh verdict: 'In Luke's opinion, the world will be much better off when "the Jews" get what they deserve and the world is rid of them.'[18]

Expectations fulfilled (but in unexpected ways): Israel transformed into the Church

What is in view in this section is not the traditional interpretation in which the rejection of the Jews and the emergence of the Gentile Church as the 'new Israel' are understood to be the fulfilment of Scripture. Instead, we are dealing here with a different – and striking – reading of Luke–Acts that has been pioneered by the Norwegian scholar Jacob Jervell. His reading overlaps with the previous one to a certain extent, in that for him Luke believes that God's dealings with Israel have come to an end and that the mission of the Church is now entirely to the Gentiles. But he arrives at this somewhat similar destination by quite a different route. Two aspects of his reading are of particular interest here – one having to do with the mission to Israel, the other with the place and character of Gentile believers.

First, Jervell argues that for Luke the apostolic mission to Israel has been a success, not a failure. Although Luke takes note of Jewish opposition to and rejection of the gospel, he goes out of his way to 'relate the great success of the Christian mission to the Jews'.[19] Peter's Pentecost sermon in Jerusalem resulted in the conversion of three thousand people (Acts 2.41) and others were added 'day by day' (2.47). The narrative to follow is punctuated with other accounts of mass conversions in Jerusalem and Judea (4.4; 5.14; 6.1, 7; 9.42; 12.24), leading up to James's reference to the 'many thousands' of Torah-observing, Jewish believers (21.20). Such results are found in the diaspora as well, as Paul's preaching repeatedly leads to the conversion of 'many' Jews (13.43; 14.1; 17.12; 19.17–20). Since a number of these

[17] Sanders, *The Jews in Luke–Acts*, 303.

[18] Ibid., 317.

[19] Jacob Jervell, *Luke and the People of God* (Minneapolis: Augsburg, 1972), 44.

passages are in the form of summary statements, they clearly reflect a deliberate emphasis on Luke's part.

According to Jervell, one cannot minimize or nullify this emphasis by appealing to the passages in which Paul says that he is turning to the Gentiles. For one thing, despite having made such a statement in one city, when Paul arrives in the next city he invariably begins by preaching to Jews (14.1; 18.19). Further, as has already been noted, at least some of his Jewish hearers respond positively wherever he goes. Even when Paul makes these statements about turning to the Gentiles, this happens only after 'many' (13.43), or 'some' (28.24–25) or at least one (18.8) of his Jewish hearers had become believers. The picture that Luke presents, then, is not of Israel's rejection but of its division: 'The picture is clear: Israel has not rejected the gospel, but has become divided over the issue.' This 'clear picture' is present even at the end of the narrative: 'some are convinced, others remain unbelieving (28.24f.)'.[20] Further, such a picture is anticipated at the outset, when Peter declares that those Jews who refuse to repent and to listen to the gospel 'will be utterly rooted out of the people' (3.23). While the unrepentant may be excluded, 'the people' – 'the descendants of the prophets and of the covenant that God gave to your ancestors' (3.25), i.e. Israel – continues to exist in the body of Jews who recognize Jesus as the Messiah (3.19), the prophet about whom Moses spoke (3.22–23). Acts 2.23 thus provides the key for understanding the rest of the story.

This leads to the second significant feature of Jervell's reading. It is the emergence of a purged and repentant Israel – not the rejection of Israel – that provides the theological justification for the Gentile mission. It is only when Israel has had a chance to hear and respond to the gospel that a way is opened for preaching to the Gentiles. This is signalled already in Acts 3. At the end of his sermon, Peter points ahead to the inclusion of the Gentiles, citing God's promise to Abraham about the blessing of 'all the families of the earth' through 'his descendants' (3.25). But 'to you first', Peter says, God has sent his servant to bring blessing to Israel 'by turning each of you from your wicked ways' (3.26). First there will be blessing for a purged and repentant Israel; only then will blessing be extended to the nations.

[20] Ibid., 49.

Jervell finds confirmation of this in James's declaration at the Jerusalem conference, where he justifies the Gentile mission on the basis of Amos 9.11–12 (quoting the Greek translation, which differs from the Hebrew): 'I will rebuild the dwelling of David, which has fallen . . . so that all other peoples may seek the Lord – even all the Gentiles over whom my name has been called' (Acts 15.16–17 NRSV). For Jervell, the reference to 'all other peoples' (literally, 'the rest of humankind') means that the rebuilding of the dwelling of David refers to the restoration of Israel itself rather than simply to the coming of the messianic 'son of David'. The intended outcome of this restoration ('so that') is the gathering of 'the Gentiles over whom my name has been called'. This reading might find confirmation in the fact that in the Greek translation the dwelling of David is said to be 'raised up' (rather than 'rebuilt'), which could have been read as a reference to the 'raising up' of Jesus from death. If Luke was aware of this version, his choice of a different term might suggest that he wanted to avoid the implication that the Gentile mission was predicated simply on the resurrection of Jesus.

Jervell finds further confirmation of his interpretation in the kind of Gentiles who 'seek the Lord' in Acts. It has often been noted that Luke shows great interest in Gentile 'God-fearers' or 'worshippers of God'; some have even argued that the category is a Lukan invention. But invention or (more probably) not, says Jervell, what has not been observed is that for Luke this is normative. Cornelius is not only the first Gentile convert but also 'the model, the prototype for every non-Jew who wants to be a member of the church'.[21] Almost invariably, the first converts in any city are those who were already attached to the synagogue. Even if this is not made explicit in every case (11.20; 17.33), the terms on which Gentiles are to be included are set at the Jerusalem council; in essence the apostolic decree (15.19–21) consists of those aspects of the law of Moses that were applicable to Gentiles and, indeed, were heard by God-fearers 'every sabbath in the synagogues'. So for Luke 'these so-called Godfearing Gentiles are the only Gentiles he finds and wants to find in the church'.[22] The Church thus includes Gentiles on the same terms as does the synagogue:

[21] Jacob Jervell, 'The Church of Jews and Godfearers', in *Luke–Acts and the Jewish People*, ed. Joseph B. Tyson (Minneapolis: Augsburg, 1988), 13.

[22] Ibid., 12.

Gentiles either are God-fearers already or they need to 'fear God and do what is right' in the same way (cf. 10.35).

In essence, then, Jervell understands Luke's narrative as an account of the fulfilment, and not the failure, of the expectations aroused at the beginning. The message of the gospel brings both 'glory to God's people Israel', in the emergence of a purged and repentant people, and 'light to the Gentiles', in the inclusion of God-fearing Gentiles in the Church (cf. Luke 2.32). For Luke, the Church itself represents the fulfilment of the prophetic expectation 'that at the end of times the Gentiles will be included in the restored Israel'.[23]

One further point needs to be noted. In Jervell's understanding of Luke's view of things, the mission to the Jews is a thing of the past. The division of Israel has been fully accomplished; a purified remnant of Israel has been gathered; only the mission to the Gentiles will continue into the future. In part, Jervell bases this on Paul's concluding speech to the Jews in Rome, with its note of finality. More fundamentally, however, his view is based on the assumption that Luke writes in a time when the Jewish mission was indeed over and the Church was making its way in the Gentile world. We will return to the question of the social location of Luke and his intended readers in the next section.

Expectations remain unfulfilled: Israel and Church in tension

While Jervell has drawn our attention to aspects of Luke–Acts that are often overlooked, his interpretation has also been subject to criticism. For example, if Luke really understood the apostolic decree as a summary of those aspects of the Mosaic law that pertain to Gentiles, he could have made it much more explicit. He makes no reference to pertinent passages of Scripture (e.g. Lev. 17.8–16); the decree is promulgated simply on the authority of 'the apostles and the elders' (Acts 15.23), with no reference to Moses. Further, if the status of Gentiles in the Church is simply an extension of something that was already an established category in the Jewish world, it is surprising that, in Luke's account of it, Peter experiences it as something new and unprecedented (10.14, 28). In addition, one cannot

[23] Jervell, *Luke and the People of God*, 53.

help but feel that the differences between the traditional Jewish expectations at the start of Luke and the fulfilment that Jervell perceives as having been accomplished by the end of Acts are so stark as to be unconvincing. Where is the restoration of the throne of David (Luke 1.32), the defeat of Israel's enemies (1.71, 74) or the 'redemption of Jerusalem' (2.38)? Who, looking on from the outside, would see the existence of a relatively small group of Jewish believers in Jesus (and even this now a thing of the past) as anything even remotely corresponding to what was usually intended by such terms? Would this not represent such a radical reinterpretation as to amount to a trivialization of Israel's hope, a desperate expedient to salvage some form of connection with the past?

This leads, however, to a third set of readings, in which Luke is seen not as having abandoned traditional Jewish expectations but as continuing to hold open some form of future hope for Israel. In part, support for such readings is found in the straightforward way in which Israel's traditional hope is presented in the first two chapters of Luke. Luke gives us no reason to believe that he doubts the validity of the expectations articulated in these chapters. Mary, Simeon, Anna and even Zechariah are treated as reliable characters. There is no hint in these chapters that Luke wants us eventually to see them as 'blinded by Jewish nationalism and by traditional assumptions of God's preference for Israel'.[24]

Further, these initial impressions of Luke's purpose seem to be reaffirmed later in the narrative in statements that assume the ongoing validity of Israel's traditional hopes for end-time redemption. Luke prefaces his account of the parable of the entrusted money (Luke 19.11–27) with the statement that Jesus told this parable to his disciples 'because he was near Jerusalem and because they supposed that the kingdom of God was to appear immediately'. Luke understands the disciples to be mistaken in their timing, but gives no indication that they were mistaken in their understanding – specifically, of a kingdom of God that would appear when the Messiah arrived in Jerusalem. On the road to Emmaus, Cleopas and his companion say to the stranger who has joined them on their

[24] Robert C. Tannehill, 'Israel in Luke–Acts: A Tragic Story', *Journal of Biblical Literature* 104 (1985): 73.

journey, 'But we had hoped that he was the one to redeem Israel' (Luke 24.21 NRSV). The statement is highly ironic, in that the disciples were unaware that their fellow traveller was none other than the supposedly failed redeemer, now raised from the dead by God. But the irony is not at the expense of their now-disappointed hope; their mistake was not the belief that Israel would be redeemed, but their belief that Jesus' death meant that he could not be Israel's redeemer. A similar note is sounded in Acts 1.6, where the disciples ask the risen Jesus, 'Lord, is this the time when you will restore the kingdom to Israel?' Again, Luke presents them as mistaken in their sense of God's timetable for restoration, but not in their expectation that Israel would be restored. Shortly after, in the second of Peter's sermons to a Jewish audience, he describes Jesus as 'the Messiah appointed for you' who will return from heaven to establish 'the time of universal restoration that God announced long ago through his holy prophets' (3.20–21 NRSV). As in the preceding passages, the expectations awakened in the early chapters of Luke concerning the consolation of Israel and the redemption of Jerusalem seem to be reaffirmed in Peter's sermon, even if their fulfilment is still a thing of the future.

Although nothing as explicit appears after Peter's statements in Acts 3.19–21, these expectations are by no means negated, not even when the narrative shifts from Peter to Paul. Perhaps surprisingly, given Paul's characterization as the 'apostle to the Gentiles', the initial narrative of his call gives equal place to Israel. God has chosen him 'to bring my name before Gentiles and kings and before the people of Israel' (9.15 NRSV). Further, even at the end of Acts, Paul can declare to the Jewish community in Rome that 'it is for the sake of the hope of Israel' that he is a prisoner there (28.20). To be sure, several previous statements might give the impression that for Paul the sphere of Israel's hope has contracted simply to the hope of resurrection and, with even a smaller radius, to the resurrection of the Messiah (23.6; 24.15, 21; 26.6–8). Still, he describes his message as consisting of 'nothing but what the prophets and Moses said would take place' – specifically, that the Messiah, after his suffering, death and resurrection, 'would proclaim light both to our people and to the Gentiles' (26.22–23 NRSV). And still, however the hope has been concentrated or re-centred, it continues to be the 'hope of Israel'. In addition, even after Paul has made his final statement about the blindness of 'this people' and the salvation of the Gentiles (28.25–28), he continues to welcome 'all who came to him' (28.29); since 'some' of his Jewish hearers had been 'convinced' by his preaching (28.24), there is no reason to suppose that it was only Gentiles who sought Paul out. In other words, no door has been shut; the mission to Israel continues even beyond the end of the narrative and into the future.

On the basis of such considerations, a number of scholars have argued that for Luke the initial expectations remain valid, even if their full consummation is yet to be realized.[25] The least optimistic of these scholars is Robert Tannehill.[26] For Tannehill, Luke perceives the story of Israel as a 'tragic' one, even if he has not fully abandoned the hope that it might in the end have a happier ending. Tannehill gives full weight to the sincerity with which the initial expectations are presented; Luke gives no indication that they are to be radically reinterpreted (e.g. as in the case of Jervell) or revoked (e.g. Sanders). Certainly the expectations have not been fulfilled; because of Israel's failure to recognize Jesus or to repent at the preaching of the apostles, Jerusalem has been destroyed and left desolate (Luke 13.33–35; 19.41–44; 21.20–24; 23.27–31). But while Luke is constrained to tell of the destruction of Jerusalem rather than of its redemption, and of the desolation of Israel rather than of its consolation, he takes no pleasure in this turn of events. It is an occasion for weeping, not for gloating: Jesus weeps over the prospect of Jerusalem's destruction (only in Luke; see 19.41) and he later urges the 'daughters of Jerusalem' to weep over the coming calamity (23.27–31). For Tannehill, there is no doubt that Luke expects his readers to do the same; 'the author is guiding the readers to experience the story of Israel and its messiah as a tragic story'.[27]

---

[25] In addition to Tannehill and Tiede (discussed below), see e.g. John Koenig, *Jews and Christians in Dialogue: New Testament Foundations* (Philadelphia: Westminster Press, 1979), 107–15; Robert L. Brawley, *Luke–Acts and the Jews: Conflict, Apology, and Conciliation* (Atlanta, Ga.: Scholars Press, 1987); David P. Moessner, 'The Ironic Fulfillment of Israel's Glory', in *Luke–Acts and the Jewish People*, ed. Joseph B. Tyson (Minneapolis: Augsburg, 1988), 35–50.

[26] Tannehill, 'Israel in Luke–Acts: A Tragic Story', 69–85; *The Narrative Unity of Luke–Acts: A Literary Interpretation* (Philadelphia: Fortress Press, 1986–90); 'Rejection by Jews and Turning to Gentiles: The Pattern of Paul's Mission in Acts', in *Luke–Acts and the Jewish People*, ed. Joseph B. Tyson (Minneapolis: Augsburg, 1988), 83–101.

[27] Tannehill, 'Israel in Luke–Acts: A Tragic Story', 74.

The tragic character of Israel's story, however, presents Luke with a theological problem. Tannehill sees indications of Luke's attempt to wrestle with the problem in the material mentioned above, where Israel's expectations are affirmed and some hope is held open that they will yet be fulfilled. He also draws attention to the temporal limitation in Luke 21.24: the desolation of Jerusalem will last only 'until the times of the Gentiles are fulfilled'. In a sense, Luke does not let tragedy have the final word. Still, Luke's willingness to hold the door open to a more optimistic ending represents not so much a solution to the problem as it is a refusal to take the easy way out: 'Living with an unresolved theological problem is a price that the author is willing to pay to remain faithful to Israel and its Scriptures.'[28]

A much more optimistic reading is found in the work of David Tiede.[29] While Tiede agrees with Tannehill about the 'poignant and potentially tragic' character of Luke's narrative,[30] he grounds his more optimistic reading on Simeon's two oracles in Luke 2.29–35, and in particular on an unexpected element of order in each. In the first oracle, Simeon mentions 'a light for revelation to the Gentiles' and then 'glory to your people Israel'; in the second, he speaks of 'the falling' and then 'of the rising of many in Israel'. Taking each of these in the sense of a temporal sequence, Tiede understands Luke to be signalling that the story he has to tell will have to do first with the fall, of Israel and the salvation of the Gentiles, and then with Israel's rise and glorification. Simeon's oracles thus 'foreshadow the entire story'[31] and provide the reader with the key to its meaning. Although Luke–Acts deals more with the fall than with the glory, Luke's readers have been primed to recognize that glory will succeed fall, and they have been given enough confirmation along the way to know that Simeon's oracles remain valid. Thus if the falling has taken place and a light of revelation has gone to the Gentiles, the inevitable outcome of the story will be Israel's rising

[28] Ibid., 84 n. 30.

[29] David L. Tiede, *Prophecy and History in Luke–Acts* (Philadelphia: Fortress Press, 1980); '"Glory to Thy People Israel": Luke–Acts and the Jews', in *Luke–Acts and the Jewish People*, ed. Joseph B. Tyson (Minneapolis: Augsburg, 1988), 21–34.

[30] Tiede, '"Glory to Thy People Israel"', 24.

[31] Ibid., 27.

and glorification – even if this outcome lies beyond the end of the narrative as we have it.

Any understanding of self-definition in Luke–Acts, then, needs to take account of several distinct but interconnected issues: (1) *The mission to Israel*: Was it a success or a failure? Has it been completed, in Luke's perspective, or is it still ongoing? Has Israel been rejected or divided? (2) *The mission to the Gentiles*: Was it made possible by Israel's rejection or was it dependent on the prior existence of a believing remnant of Israel? Do Gentile believers replace (unrepentant) Jews or are they added to a Jewish remnant? (3) *The relative place of Jew and Gentile in the Church*: Do Jewish Christians somehow represent the continuation of Israel? Is 'God-fearing' the model for Gentile Christians? More generally, do the categories 'Jew' and 'Gentile' have continuing significance? Were they significant only for a transitional period in the past? Or have they been fundamentally transcended from the outset? (4) *The future of Israel*: Does Luke hold open any hope for the redemption of Israel as Israel in the messianic future, or is hope limited to the possibility of conversion to Christ in the present?

As was the case with Matthew, Luke–Acts contains material that might be taken to support one or other of the options in each case, resulting in quite distinct constructions of Christian identity. Once again, however, decisions concerning questions of self-definition cannot be made in isolation, but need to be correlated with questions concerning social location and rhetorical intent.

Social location of Luke and his intended readers

How we assess the treatment of Jews and Judaism within the narrative world of Luke–Acts will depend on how we perceive several aspects of the historical world within which the narrative came to be – namely, Luke's ethnic identity, the social situation and character of his own Christian community, and the identity of his intended readers. We have very little in the way of firm external evidence, however, which means that for the most part we are thrown back onto Luke–Acts itself and thus onto the material surveyed in the previous section. For this reason, we do not need an extended discussion here.

We will begin with Luke himself. Here we will not concern ourselves with the debate as to whether the author of Luke–Acts is to be identified with Luke, 'the beloved physician' and sometime companion of Paul (Philem. 24; Col. 4.14). If the debate could be resolved in the affirmative, it would indicate that the author was Gentile, since according to Colossians 4.10–14, Luke belongs to a group of Paul's co-workers who are not 'of the circumcision'. But this would not take us very far, since there is widespread agreement that the author of a narrative that displays such interest in Gentiles and the Gentile mission must have been Gentile himself.

To be sure, the author displays an interest in the Jewish world as well. He is very familiar with the Scriptures of Israel (in Greek) and is able to write in a style reminiscent of biblical Greek. Most of the non-Christian Gentiles in his narrative stand in some sort of relationship with the Jewish community (as proselytes or as 'God-fearers'). As for the Christian Gentiles, they appear in a narrative that places the Gentile mission squarely in a Jewish context, as Luke is evidently concerned to show how the Gentile mission was able to overcome Jewish-Christian reservations and to succeed in spite of Jewish opposition. Although such considerations by no means imply that Luke was Jewish, they have led some interpreters to argue that he himself had been attracted to Judaism before he became a Christ-believer – in other words, that he had been the kind of 'God-fearer' that he later came to write about in his narrative. Still, such a conclusion is no more than plausible, and even this depends to some extent on conclusions concerning self-definition in Luke–Acts. The more Luke–Acts is read in an anti-Jewish way as a story of rejection and replacement, the less likely it is that it was written by someone who saw in a Cornelius a reflection of his own experience.

Further, the plausibility of such a conclusion depends on whether the situation described in Acts – a mixed Church of Jews and Gentiles, many of whom had already been synagogue adherents – reflects the circumstances in Luke's own day, or whether he was looking back on a transitional situation now very much a thing of the past. What then of Luke's own situation?

To begin with, when did he write? Luke's narrative breaks off with Paul in Rome, under house arrest while he waits for his case to be heard. Although Paul has been taken to Rome precisely so that he can appeal his case to Caesar, the author tells us nothing about the outcome. For this reason, a few scholars have argued that the date of composition of Luke–Acts was sometime in the 60s, while Paul was still a Roman prisoner.[32] However, the farewell speech that Paul delivers to the elders of the church in Ephesus (Acts 20.18–35) seems to betray an awareness that Paul did die and that certain problems developed in the church after his death. Further, the prophecy of the fall of Jerusalem (Luke 21.20–24) contains details not present in Mark or Matthew (e.g. 'Jerusalem surrounded by armies', v. 20; 'Jerusalem . . . trampled on by the Gentiles', v. 24) that seem to reflect what actually happened in the war with Rome (70 CE). Acts is by no means a biography of Paul. Luke may well have felt that his narrative purposes were accomplished with the arrival of the gospel in Rome and expected that most of his readers, already aware of Paul's death, could readily supply the ending to the story of Paul. Thus a majority of scholars place the writing of Acts considerably later than the date of the last narrated event – perhaps in the 80s or 90s,[33] or even as late as the early second century.[34] Again, if we could identify the author of Luke–Acts with Luke, the companion of Paul, we could narrow the options, since, if this were the case, a second-century date would be highly unlikely. But the two issues are interrelated, which means that we cannot use the one (the issue of authorship) to limit the options for the other (date).

Our immediate question concerns the social character and situation of the Church in Luke's own day. Luke presents the history of the Church – from its beginnings as an entirely Jewish movement in Jerusalem under the leadership of Peter, through the emergence of the Gentile mission, to the arrival of Paul in Rome and his sojourn there – as a smooth and harmonious development, guided by God and affirmed by all the major participants in the story. Of course, we are aware from Paul's letters that the progression was much bumpier and that there was considerable tension between Paul and 'those who were already apostles before' him (Gal. 1.17), tensions that are readily apparent in Acts, despite Luke's emphasis on harmony and progressive development. Are we to imagine that Luke wrote in a

---

32 E.g. F. F. Bruce, *Commentary on the Book of the Acts* (Grand Rapids: Eerdmans, 1975), 21–3.

33 C. K. Barrett, *A Critical and Exegetical Commentary on the Acts of the Apostles*, vol. 2 (Edinburgh: T&T Clark, 1998), xlii.

34 E.g. Helmut Koester, *Introduction to the New Testament*, vol. 2: *History and Literature of Early Christianity* (Philadelphia: Fortress Press, 1982), 310.

situation where there was still considerable tension between Jewish Christians who identified themselves with James or Peter on the one hand, and those who looked to Paul as their apostolic model on the other? If so, was Luke squarely in one of the camps (presumably Pauline Christianity) or, given his positive treatment of all three, was he representative of some mediating group? Or does his positive treatment of all three suggest that he wrote in a later period where these earlier tensions were a thing of the past and a new consensus (sometimes described as early catholicism) was in the making? If so, might we take this one step further and see in the 'savage wolves' that come into the Church (Acts 20.29) or that emerge from within it (20.30) an early reflection of the tendencies that developed into Marcionism or the various forms of Gnosticism? Or was it the case that the primary tensions facing Luke's church were those that stemmed from the synagogue down the street or the representatives of Roman imperial power?

As was the case with Matthew, how we assess Luke's treatment of Israel and the Jewish people will vary with the answers that might be given to these questions about his own ethnic identity, the ethnic makeup of the church with which he identified, and its relationship with other groups within and outside the Christian movement. Answers to these questions, in turn, will depend on how we understand Luke's purposes with respect to his intended readership.

Rhetorical function of Luke's treatment of Jews and Judaism

Unlike the other evangelists, Luke begins with a prologue (Luke 1.1–4) in which he both identifies his intended reader ('I too decided . . . to write an orderly account for you, most excellent Theophilus') and states his purpose in writing ('so that you may know the truth concerning the things about which you have been instructed/informed' NRSV). This prologue, though of considerable significance, is sufficiently ambiguous at key points that it is open to a variety of interpretations.

The first point of ambiguity concerns Theophilus. It probably can be taken for granted that Luke did not write solely for the benefit of a single individual but that he expected others to be reading over Theophilus' shoulder. But how are we to identify Theophilus and the group that he represents? Since it was a common practice in Luke's day to address a work to a patron or other prominent individual (for example, the Epaphroditus to whom Josephus addresses his *Against Apion*), it is possible that we are to understand Theophilus as just such an individual, so that Luke was addressing his work to a real person of eminence as a way of attracting a certain circle of readers. The fact that Luke uses 'excellent' (*kratiste*) on three occasions in Acts as a term of address for a Roman governor (23.26; 24.3; 26.25) suggests the possibility that he was addressing his two-volume account of Christian origins to an outside readership, a circle of literate Romans who might have (or who might be persuaded to have) some sympathies for the Christian movement. At the same time, however, the name Theophilus – literally, 'loving God' or 'loved by God' – is highly suggestive. Perhaps Theophilus functions for Luke as an ideal figure, a stand-in for all who might see themselves (or who might be persuaded to see themselves) as loved by or loving God.

The second point of ambiguity concerns Luke's statement of purpose. Has Theophilus merely been 'informed' about the Christian story, which would make him an interested outsider? Or has he been 'instructed' in the Christian way, which would identify him as a Christian insider or at least as one on his way to full conversion? The verb *katēcheō* could have either meaning, with the result that Luke could conceivably have had either group of intended readers in mind.

Any resolution of these questions will depend, then, on our assessment of the work as a whole and the purpose that seems to be implicit in it. Before looking at the variety of answers that have been suggested, we should begin by noting a number of features of Luke–Acts that are generally recognized and that have some bearing on the question of purpose.

First, there can be little doubt that Luke intended his two-volume work to be seen as a kind of history. The term by which he describes his work (*diēgēsis*; Luke 1.1) was often used with reference to historical narrative (e.g. Josephus, *Life of Josephus* 336). Other elements – the further description of the work as having to do with 'the things that have come to fulfilment among us' (Luke 1.1), the formal address to a patron, the lengthy chronological and political introduction to the ministry of John the Baptist (Luke 3.1–2) and the general concern for orderly progression – all point in this direction. In addition, this history was intended to serve as a means of persuasion: Luke wanted

Theophilus to know the 'certainty' (*asphaleia*; Luke 1.4) of the story, to have secure knowledge about it. Luke–Acts can be described, then, as apologetic history.[35]

Second, we can identify a number of themes and emphases that evidently play a role in Luke's persuasive case. For one thing, there can be little doubt that Luke wanted to present the Church as standing in continuity with the story of Israel and as the legitimate heir of its Scripture and tradition. 'What God had promised' to Israel of old God has fulfilled for the 'descendants of Abraham's family and others who fear God' 'by raising Jesus from the dead' (Acts 13.32, 26, 33). For another, as an aspect of this continuation and fulfilment, he also wanted to argue for the legitimacy of the inclusion of the Gentiles and the movement into the Roman world. This movement is both anticipated in Scripture (15.15–18) and brought about by divine agency (Acts 10.34–35, 45–47; 11.17–18; 15.7–9; 26.16–18). Further, Luke was clearly aware of the anxieties that arose because of the delay of Jesus' return (or parousia) and the full establishment of God's reign (Luke 19.11; Acts 1.6), and his decision to devote a separate volume to the life of the Church seems to reflect a concern to establish a distinct period for the Church within 'the times or periods that the Father has set by his own authority' (Acts 1.7). In addition, while conflict and controversy might have attended the spread of the Christian way, Luke went out of his way to present the Roman empire, in the persons of its local representatives, as fair and even-handed, ready to acknowledge that Christianity did not represent any intrinsic threat to the well-being of the empire (13.7–12; 16.35–39; 18.12–16; 19.35–41; 21.37–40; 22.23–29; 23.16–30; 25.13–27; 26.30–32; 27.42–44). Finally, since Luke devoted more than half of the Acts account to Paul, it is clear that he saw Paul as 'an instrument whom [God has] chosen to bring [God's] name before Gentiles and kings and before the people of Israel' (9.15 NRSV). At the same time, however, Luke downplayed any differences between Paul and the original apostles, presenting them as in agreement concerning both the legitimacy of the Gentile mission (Acts 10–11; 15.7–21) and the continuing importance of Torah observance for Jewish believers

---

[35] See e.g. Gregory E. Sterling, *Historiography and Self-Definition: Josephos, Luke–Acts, and Apologetic Historiography*, Supplements to Novum Testamentum 64 (Leiden and New York: Brill, 1992).

(21.20–26). Peter, James and Paul form a united front in the ongoing progression of God's plans and purposes.

Still, these widely recognized features of Luke–Acts can be – and indeed have been – aligned with a variety of assessments of Luke's rhetorical purpose with respect to his intended readership. One set of opinions sees Luke–Acts as addressed to outsiders. An older view, that Acts (at least) was written by a companion of Paul as a document for the defence at his trial in Rome, no longer finds adherents. But extending and broadening the scope, it is still possible to argue that Luke was addressing those who shaped or influenced Roman policy, in order to persuade them of the legitimacy and political innocuousness of the new movement. The element of newness, actually, was part of the problem. With their reverence for antiquity and adherence to tradition, the Romans would have had an innate suspicion of a movement that could claim no long-standing tradition, but was grounded in work of a recent teacher – one, moreover, who had been executed by the Romans themselves. To be sure, as long as the Christian movement was seen as just an aspect of Judaism, Roman suspicion would not have been aroused, for they had learned to accommodate Jewish distinctiveness (including their refusal to honour the gods of the empire), partly because they recognized this as loyalty to ancestral tradition and admired the Jews for it. But as soon as Rome began to perceive the Christians as an entity distinct from Judaism, they were no longer able to benefit from this policy of tolerance. Luke–Acts could be read as an attempt to persuade Theophilus, and highly placed Romans like him, that the Christian movement was the legitimate continuation of the people of Israel and thus deserving of a similar degree of tolerance.

If this was Luke's purpose, then while he would have needed to defend the legitimacy of the movement against Jewish opposition, his critique of the Jews would have been subject to significant constraints. To de-legitimize Jews and Judaism in any fundamental way would have undermined Roman tolerance of 'the people of Israel' in any form, and thus would have worked against Luke's own interests. In this reading of Luke–Acts, then, his criticism of 'the Jews' should probably be seen as playing a restricted role and as directed primarily against instances of Jewish intolerance.

It is perhaps difficult to imagine, however, that Luke would have expected any Roman official to plough through such a long and (on this view) largely tangential account in order to discern an appeal for tolerance, especially an account that begins on such a revolutionary note ('he has brought down the powerful from their thrones'; Luke 1.52 NRSV). Another way of construing the person of Theophilus is to see him as a potential Gentile convert. As the Christian movement began to make its way in the Gentile world and to seek new adherents, it would need to address questions that would be posed by any intelligent Gentiles. Why are there two groups (Jewish synagogues and Gentile churches) laying claim to the same God and the same tradition? What claim do these new non-Jewish communities have to the Scriptures and tradition of Israel? Is there any legitimacy to the Christian claim whatsoever? The second-century writer Celsus was certainly not the first to ask such questions. Theophilus could be seen as a stand-in for any potential 'lover of God' who had been informed about the movement and who might even have been attracted to it, but for whom such questions stood as an obstacle to conversion.

Reading Luke–Acts as an appeal to Gentile outsiders for conversion rather than for tolerance would raise the possibility that Luke's treatment of Jews and Judaism not only was anti-Judaic but also played a more prominent and categorical role, one aimed at denouncing the Jews and de-legitimizing their religious identity. The role would be analogous to the later Christian writings 'against the Jews', so that the closer we align Luke with the social location of, say, Justin Martyr, the more anti-Judaic and even potentially antisemitic he becomes.

Such questions would not have been limited to outsiders or potential converts, however. Christian insiders could also have felt their force, especially as time went on and the pertinent factors – the delay of the parousia, the lack of response from Jews, the increasingly Gentile character of the Church – became more pronounced. Jewish Christians for their part may well have had questions about God's purposes vis-à-vis Israel: Has God abandoned Israel and turned to the Gentiles instead? Does the coming of Jesus mean that the story of God's dealings with Israel is a story that ends in tragedy? What about the promises, 'the oath that God swore to our ancestor Abraham'? Gentile Christians might ask similar questions from a slightly different perspective: Can this God be trusted? If God's dealings with Israel have come to such a sad and sorry end, what is to say that the same thing won't happen with us Gentiles? Alternatively, Gentile Christians might respond with a kind of haughty disdain for the Jewish roots of the Church (cf. Rom. 11.17–24), even feeling – as did Marcion a little later – that the Church would be better off without all this Jewish 'baggage'. In various ways, then, Luke can be understood as having written with a pastoral and theological purpose – to address questions or concerns that might have been unsettling for the various Theophiluses in his church and to provide them with assurance 'concerning the things about which [they had] been instructed'.

If this was Luke's purpose, our assessment of the possibly anti-Jewish material in his work will depend on the social character of the church to which he addressed himself. If he wrote in a time when there was still a sizeable Jewish-Christian community to which he was positively disposed, then even if he himself were Gentile, his criticism of Jews and Judaism could be seen as much less anti-Judaic or potentially antisemitic than if he wrote in a time when the Jewish mission was a thing of the past and his church was largely Gentile.

Concluding observations

Is Luke–Acts antisemitic? anti-Judaic? supersessionistic? As was the case with Matthew, our answer to these questions depends on where we locate Luke–Acts on our three-dimensional grid (self-definition, social location and rhetorical function). While many of the considerations are similar, Luke–Acts also presents us with different or additional factors: the two-part character of the work, the Gospel being supplemented by a second volume dealing with the spread of the Church from Jerusalem to Rome and the transition of the Church's mission from Jews to Gentiles; the probability of Gentile authorship; the possibility that the work was addressed to outsiders, with an apologetic or evangelistic purpose, rather than to Christian insiders. However, as with Matthew there is a range of possibilities as to where Luke–Acts is to be located on this three-dimensional grid, and thus a range of possible answers to the questions. And again, the overall assessment of Luke's treatment of Jews and Judaism will depend on the cumulative result of the decisions that interpreters need to make along each of these axes.

4

John

> You are from your father the devil, and you choose to do your father's desires. He was a murderer from the beginning.
>
> (John 8.44 NRSV)

In chapters 7 and 8 of John's Gospel, we are presented with an extended scene in which Jesus is engaged in teaching and, consequently, in conflict with some of his hearers over the substance of his teaching. To this extent, at least, the scene resembles analogous passages in the Synoptic Gospels. In most respects, however, a reader is struck by the differences. While the event takes place long before the 'triumphal entry', it happens not in Galilee but in the Jerusalem Temple. What provokes conflict is not Jesus' attitude towards the law of Moses but his self-claim as the one sent by his Father ('If you knew me, you would know my Father also'; 8.19 NRSV). The most striking difference, however, has to do with John's characterization of Jesus' opponents. While John is well aware that Jesus' opponents included the Pharisees and the chief priests (7.32, 45; 8.13), and while he also recognizes that some of the Jewish crowd responded positively to Jesus (7.40, 43; 8.31), he nevertheless routinely refers to Jesus' opponents simply and without differentiation as 'the Jews' (7.1, 11, 13, 15; 8.48, 52). Further, a defining characteristic of 'the Jews' for John is their long-standing desire to kill Jesus (7.1; 8.37, 40, 59; also 7.19, 25). Even more disturbingly, the reason for this murderous intent is that the 'father' of 'the Jews' is not (as they claimed) Abraham (8.39) or even God (8.41), but 'the devil', who 'was a murderer from the beginning' (8.44 NRSV). Jesus and 'the Jews' are located in two distinct and opposing spheres: Jesus, whose Father is God, is 'from above', the realm of truth and light; the Jews, whose father is the devil, are 'from below', the realm of lies, murder and darkness (8.12, 23, 44).

Jules Isaac's most extensive treatment of John's Gospel appears in a section where he develops the historical argument that, in contrast to their leaders, the common Jewish people responded positively to

Jesus, which means that one cannot speak of a general rejection of Jesus on the part of the Jewish people as a whole. He admits that the argument is more easily made in the case of the Synoptic Gospels than of John, where the issue seems to have been decided even 'before we get beyond the Prologue: "He came unto his own, and his own received him not"' (1.11). Nevertheless, Isaac argues that, despite the evangelist's own intentions, the same 'historic reality' that we see in the Synoptics shines through the veneer of John's theological dogma.[1] In support of the argument, Isaac points to a number of passages where 'Jews' are said to believe in Jesus or, at least, to respond in positive ways.[2] He is particularly taken by the mix of historical reality and theological veneer in John 7.11–13. Here John presents a (Jewish) crowd in Jerusalem that was mixed in its opinion: some saw Jesus as 'a good man', others as a deceiver (7.11). But, the evangelist concludes, 'no one would speak openly about him for fear of the Jews' (7.13 NRSV). Isaac describes this as 'an incoherent and absurd text'. The people who feared 'the Jews' were Jews themselves. The statement is akin to saying of French crowds in Paris: 'Yet for fear of the French . . . no one (among the Parisians or French) spoke openly of Joan of Arc.'[3]

For Isaac, the absurdity of this passage epitomizes tensions running through the Gospel as a whole. John 'speaks of the Jews rather as if he were speaking of an alien people, alien to Jesus and his disciples, alien to John himself'[4] – alien, that is, to people who are also Jews themselves. How to account for this? Isaac rejects the idea that the evangelist himself was Gentile. Instead, this puzzling usage points to John's theological intentions in his own historical situation. Like Matthew, John wrote in a period of tension and hostility after the war with Rome. During this period, the Church, recognizing 'how greatly it was to its advantage to detach itself from the Jews', was separating itself from the synagogue, with the result that the two 'became adversaries, sometimes (the theologians especially, the

[1] Jules Isaac, *Jesus and Israel* (New York: Holt, Rinehart & Winston, 1971), 110–11.

[2] He lists the following (pp. 120–1): 2.23; 6.14, 24, 30; 7.31, 40–41, 43, 45, 47–49; 8.30; 11.45, 47–48; 12.9–11, 19, 42.

[3] Ibid., 115.

[4] Ibid., 112.

doctors) mortal enemies'.[5] In this context and 'with a view to burning his bridges behind him and to moving the Christian secession wholly beyond recall', John decided 'to treat the Jewish people as aliens, and even more as an enemy, to mark their name with a sort of brand'.[6] While careful readers might be able to see through this theological veneer, it is not surprising that most of John's readers through the centuries have been unable to distinguish between 'Jews' and 'Jews', and have thus ended up 'feeling an overwhelming aversion to the Jewish people in toto'.[7]

Gregory Baum also recognizes that many generations of John's readers have perceived the Gospel as encouraging them to look with contempt on the Jewish people. He believes, however, that this perception is the result of 'careless' reading; 'John's alleged antisemitism is only apparent'.[8]

Like Isaac, Baum notes the contrast between John's use of 'the Jews' (which might lead one to forget that Jesus, his mother and his followers were also Jews) and the underlying story, which has to do with a division within the Jewish people over Jesus and his ministry. He notes the apparent incomprehensibility of 7.11–13, but he is even more struck by Jesus' statement in 13.33 ('As I said to the Jews') – 'a most curious sentence when one considers that in the whole gospel the Lord never addressed a single word to a Gentile'.[9] Also like Isaac, Baum wants to account for these peculiarities by looking to the circumstances in the period following the war with Rome, during which the Gospel was produced. Unlike Isaac, however, he sees the decisive action as having been taken by the synagogue, not by the Christians. During this period the Pharisaic leaders of the synagogue attempted to solidify their position by imposing greater uniformity on Jewish life and practice and, where necessary, by taking measures to exclude those who would not conform. Many of these measures were aimed at Christians specifically, part of 'a relentless and uncompromising struggle against the Christians living in their midst'. The

[5] Ibid., 293.

[6] Ibid., 113.

[7] Ibid., 116.

[8] Gregory Baum, *The Jews and the Gospel: A Re-Examination of the New Testament* (Westminster, Md.: Newman Press, 1961), 103, 99.

[9] Ibid., 102, 98. This assumes that both the 'royal official' of 4.46 and the 'Greeks' of 12.20 were Jews; it also excludes Jesus' conversations with Pilate.

most decisive measure was the insertion into the daily synagogue prayers (the Eighteen Benedictions) of a petition against the *minim* ('the followers of heretical sects'), which had the effect of excluding Christians from the synagogue. For Baum, this meant that from the perspective of official Judaism, it was no longer possible to be a Christian and a Jew. From John's perspective, this meant that '[t]he Synagogue had said its final "no" to Christ'.[10] This 'official repudiation of Christ on the part of the Synagogue',[11] then, provides the interpretive lens through which John perceives and presents the story of Jesus. With the assistance of hindsight, John sees these later developments as already present in earlier events, and so tells the story of Jesus in such a way that the intervening history is collapsed and the later 'repudiation of Christ' is imposed on the story.

Baum's approach is similar to that of Isaac in that, for both, John's account is one in which a later theological perspective overlays a story set in an earlier time. Nevertheless, he differs with Isaac at a number of points. One has to do with intent. Unlike Isaac, who understands John to have set out deliberately to burn the bridges between his community and the rest of the Jewish world, Baum argues that the bridges had already been burned from the other side. In his view, the Gospel needs to be read as a response to a painful exclusion rather than as an attempt to force and hasten a separation.

Another difference has to do with the collapse of the distance between the time of Jesus and John's own day. For Baum, this foreshortening is not arbitrary, but is rooted in John's belief that in Jesus' person and ministry the divinely intended fulfilment of history has reached its culmination. The judgement expected at the end of history has already appeared in its decisive form with the ministry of Jesus, even if the effects of this judgement continued to work themselves out in the course of subsequent history. A primary characteristic of this judgement is the separation it creates between those who walk in darkness and those who are children of the light (8.12; 12.35–36), between Jesus' opponents, who are 'of this world' (8.23) and who thus share in the world's hatred of Jesus (7.7), and his followers, who are 'not of the world' (15.19). At the level of the

[10] Ibid., 106.
[11] Ibid., 107.

story, those who oppose and reject Jesus are 'the Jews', the term reflecting John's awareness that official Judaism, in the form of the leaders of the synagogue, had in his own day formally rejected the Christian message. But at the level of John's theology 'the Jews' represent and stand for the more universal phenomenon of 'the world' in its opposition to God. John's real target here is not the Jewish people per se but 'the world' – 'that is, the realm of human and satanic wickedness'.[12]

In contrast to Baum, who uses John's alignment between 'the Jews' and 'the world' to soften the force of John's apparently anti-Judaic statements, Ruether sees this alignment as a measure of John's demonization of the Jewish people. She treats Paul, Hebrews and John together, as representatives of a development in which the early christological interpretation of Scripture was transposed into a philosophical and metaphysical framework. In this development, 'the antithesis between the true and the apostate Israel [is incorporated] into a world view that fuses Platonic dualism (the material and the spiritual) with messianic dualism ("this age" and the "age to come")'.[13] This development reaches its peak in John's Gospel, with its sharp dualistic contrasts between light and darkness, truth and falsehood, above and below, those of the world and those not of the world, and so on. The fact that 'the Jews' are aligned with the negative side of these pairs means that John treats the Jewish people as 'the very incarnation of the false, apostate principle of the fallen world, alienated from its true being in God'.[14] Far from softening the impact of John's statements about 'the Jews', this alignment intensifies it by putting these statements into a cosmic and dualistic framework. Thus 'John gives the ultimate theological form to that diabolizing of "the Jews" which is the root of anti-Semitism in the Christian tradition'.[15]

Self-definition in John

As Isaac, Baum and Ruether have each observed, John's choice of vocabulary has the effect of setting up a certain distance between his

[12] Ibid., 124.

[13] Rosemary R. Ruether, *Faith and Fratricide: The Theological Roots of Anti-Semitism* (Minneapolis: Seabury, 1974), 95.

[14] Ibid., 113.

[15] Ibid., 116.

intended readers and 'the Jews', thus suggesting that it was written for readers who defined themselves – or who were being encouraged to define themselves – as something other than 'Jews'. This means that John's use of 'the Jews' is related to the larger issue of self-definition in the Gospel and thus needs to be understood within this context.[16]

Indeed, even before 'the Jews' first appear on the scene (1.19), John might be understood as preparing his readers for an ethnic-specific story of rejection and replacement. Though Jesus came into the world as the true light (1.9), 'his own people did not accept him. But to all who received him, who believed in his name, he gave power to become children of God' (1.11–12 NRSV). While no further information is given here about Jesus' 'own people' (*hoi idioi*, literally, 'his own', the masculine form implying that it refers to people, not things; the latter is the sense of the neuter form *ta idia* earlier in v. 11), their identity seems to be indicated a few verses later by the contrast drawn between Moses, through whom the law was given, and Jesus Christ, the source of 'grace and truth' (1.17). Jesus' 'own people', the ones who rejected him, seem to be the people to whom the law was given – that is, the people of Israel, the Jews. The implication seems to be that those who did receive Jesus, who thereby became children of God and recipients of grace and truth, are something other than Jews.

We need to enquire, then, into the characterization and identity that John ascribes to the community of Jesus' followers. While the implied contrast with 'the Jews' is not the only pertinent factor, it is nevertheless the obvious place to begin.

'The Jews'

As has already been observed, John differs from the Synoptic Gospels both in the frequency with which he uses the term and also in its negative character. While the term is rare in the first three Gospels (five occurrences each in Matthew and Luke, six in Mark), it is found some seventy times in John. In the Synoptics 'the Jews' either is used

[16] Again it is to be noted that the name John is used for convenience. In the Gospel itself the author is identified as 'the disciple whom Jesus loved' (21.20–25), and we will later see that there are good reasons to doubt that this disciple was one of the Twelve.

by Gentiles (e.g. Matt. 2.2; Mark 15.18) or appears in a context where a Gentile perspective is included or implied (e.g. Mark 7.3; Luke 7.3), which indicates the Jew–Gentile contrast that hovers about the term and which, in turn, underlines the sense of alienation between believers and the Jewish world in John. Further, in situations of conflict and opposition, John's indiscriminate and categorical use of 'the Jews' stands in sharp contrast to the Synoptics, with their more specific designations. For example, in both the Synoptics (e.g. Mark 3.1–6 and parallels) and John (5.1–18; ch. 9) Jesus is criticized for healing on the sabbath. But while in the Synoptics the opponents are clearly designated as 'the Pharisees' (Matt. 12.14; Mark 3.6) or 'the scribes and the Pharisees' (Luke 6.7), in John they are almost always 'the Jews'. It was 'the Jews' who challenged the man who was healed (5.10) and who 'persecuted Jesus because he healed on the sabbath' (5.16), or who doubted the healing of the blind man (9.18) and who expelled him from the synagogue (9.22, 34). Or again, in the account of Jesus' trial, while in the Synoptics Jesus' accusers are the 'chief priests, the elders and scribes and the whole council' (e.g. Mark 15.1), in John it is 'the Jews' who push Pilate for a death sentence (18.31), who cry for Barabbas (18.38–40), who proclaim Jesus guilty of death (19.7) and who choose Caesar rather than Jesus as their king (19.12). To be sure, in both sets of passages John can occasionally use more specific terms: 'the Pharisees' (9.13); 'the chief priests and the Pharisees' (18.3); 'the chief priests' (19.6). While this is something that will require further attention, for present purposes it simply underlines the deliberate character of John's usage: while he was well aware that other terms could be used, most frequently he chose to describe Jesus' opponents simply as 'the Jews'.

But John's differences with the Synoptics go beyond the simple choice of a general term over more specific ones. First, John sharply accentuates the nature and the extent of the hostility of 'the Jews' towards Jesus. Not only did they persecute him, but right from the beginning of his ministry they sought to kill him (5.18; 7.1; 8.40) or to stone him (8.59; 10.31–33; 11.7–8). Further and more significantly, this murderous desire, as we have seen, is caught up into a dualistic scheme, where 'the Jews' are aligned with their 'father the devil', 'who was a murderer from the beginning' (8.44; see also vv. 21–59). It is not without significance that shortly after the first reference to the desire of 'the Jews' to kill Jesus (5.18), Jesus declares to them: 'I have come in my Father's name, and you do not receive me' (5.43). This statement both confirms and clarifies the impression created at the outset of the Gospel (1.11–12) about the identity of those (Jesus' 'own') who were not willing to 'receive' Jesus – that is, they are 'the Jews' – and it points ahead to the underlying reason – their father is not the Father of Jesus, but the devil. This seems to suggest that John's story of rejection and replacement is not only ethnic-specific (that is, a story in which a Gentile Church is seen as taking the place of the Jewish people) but also dualistic (that is, a story in which 'the Jews' are categorically associated with cosmic forces of darkness, sin and evil).

If this were the end of the matter, the picture would be bleak indeed. However, this does not exhaust what John has to say about 'the Jews'. His use of the term is by no means unrelentingly negative.

First, in at least a dozen places, the term appears in a purely neutral sense, referring to various festivals (2.13; 6.4; 7.2; 11.55) or customs (2.6; 19.40) or leaders (3.1; 18.33; 19.3, 19, 21) 'of the Jews', or to the Jews as distinct from the Samaritans (4.9). Here the term functions simply to designate the Jews as one nation or ethnic group as distinct from others. Second, the response of 'the Jews' to Jesus is not exclusively one of opposition and disbelief. On several occasions John says that 'many of the Jews believed in him' (11.45; also 8.30–31). Similar references to the 'many' who 'believed in him' appear in contexts where it is clear that the believers are Jewish, even if the term does not appear (2.23; 7.31; 10.42). The result of such belief is that 'the Jews' were divided about Jesus: 'Again there was a division among the Jews', we read in 10.19. The fact that this was not the first such instance ('again') suggests that we should see an implicit reference to 'the Jews' in earlier statements about a division – 'in the crowd' (7.43) or between 'some of the Pharisees' and 'others' (9.16) – or incidents where some speak negatively about Jesus and others positively ('a good man' (7.12); 'the prophet' or 'the Messiah' (7.40–41)). Indeed, what prompted the religious authorities finally to arrest Jesus was the fear that the positive side of this division would increase to the point that 'everyone' in 'our nation' would 'believe in him' (11.48). Third, the term is used in an even more positive sense in chapter 4, where not only does the Samaritan woman refer to Jesus himself as a Jew (v. 9; the editorial comment implying that John fully accepted the reference) but Jesus declares that 'salvation is from the Jews'

(v. 22). Jesus' identity as a Jew is also affirmed by Pilate, who speaks of Jesus' 'own nation' even as he declares that he, by contrast, is not a Jew (18.35). Finally, it is not without significance that John also uses 'Israel' without any negative overtone at all. The purpose of John the Baptist's ministry was that Jesus 'might be revealed to Israel' (1.31). Jesus describes Nathanael as 'an Israelite in whom there is no deceit' (1.47 NRSV) and says to Nicodemus that as 'a teacher of Israel' he should know all about being born of the Spirit (3.10). Jesus himself is acclaimed by Nathanael (1.49) and the Jerusalem crowds (12.13) as the 'king of Israel'.

John is thus fully aware that not all Jews fit the negative profile of 'the Jews'. Who then are these 'Jews' who refused to believe in Jesus and sought to put him to death? There are some indications that when John uses 'the Jews' in a pejorative way he has in mind a smaller group within the Jewish people as a whole.

First, on two or three occasions the term seems to be limited geographically, so that 'the Jews' are to be found in Judea, rather than in Galilee or other places where Jewish people might be found. In 7.1, where we read that Jesus 'went about in Galilee', John adds: 'He did not wish to go about in Judea because the Jews were looking for an opportunity to kill him' (NRSV). We find a similar occurrence in 11.7–8. Having left Judea for the region on the other side of the Jordan, Jesus said to his disciples: 'Let us go to Judea again'. The disciples raised objections: 'Rabbi, the Jews were just now trying to stone you [cf. 10.31], and are you going there again?' (NRSV). In both cases, murderous 'Jews' seem to be restricted to Judea – and even to Jerusalem, since Jerusalem and the Temple are central to both contexts (see 7.2, 14; 10.22). Further, the reference in 4.44 to the lack of honour ascribed to a prophet in his 'own' country might also be taken as a reference to Judea, since the passage goes on to describe the warm welcome Jesus received in Galilee.

Second, in a number of the pejorative instances, 'the Jews' seem to be virtually identified with the religious authorities in Jerusalem. In John 1.19, for example, where John the Baptist is being questioned by 'priests and Levites from Jerusalem', it is said that they had been sent by 'the Jews'. A few short verses later we read that 'they had been sent from the Pharisees' (1.24). We find a similar shift of designation in several other passages where John refers to the same group of people as 'the Jews' at one point in the account (9.18; 11.45, 54; 19.7) and as 'the Pharisees' (9.13), or 'the chief priests and the Pharisees' (11.47) or 'the chief priests and the police' (19.6) at another. Again, in chapter 9 the parents of the man born blind are reluctant to talk because 'they feared the Jews, for the Jews had already agreed that anyone who confessed Jesus to be the Messiah would be put out of the synagogue' (9.22; other references to 'fear of the Jews' in 7.13 and 19.42). In 12.42, however, fear of being put out of the synagogue is directed at the Pharisees. Related to this perhaps is the distinction that seems to be apparent in 7.10–13 between the crowds, at least some of whom thought that Jesus was a good man, and 'the Jews', who were looking for Jesus and who created fear among those who otherwise might have spoken openly about him.

To be sure, neither of these distinctions is carried through consistently. Jesus can encounter hostile 'Jews' in Galilee (6.41–52); some of the religious leaders were counted among those who believed in him (12.42; also Nicodemus (3.1–15; 7.50–52; 19.38–42)). Still, there is some indication that the closer one gets to Jerusalem, and the closer one gets to the Pharisees and chief priests, the greater the likelihood of encountering 'the Jews', in John's distinctly pejorative sense of the term.

Gentiles

But John's use of 'the Jews' is not the only indicator of self-definition in the Fourth Gospel. For generations of subsequent readers, John's negative depiction of 'the Jews' has been taken to imply, almost by definition, a positive disposition towards Gentiles. Indeed, as we have already noted, even in the first century the term 'Jews' was most at home in the Gentile world or in Jewish usage where a wider Gentile context was in view.[17] What, then, is John's attitude towards the Gentiles?

In reading the Gospel with this question in view, one is struck – at least initially – with the absence of Gentiles in John's world. The usual Jewish term – Gentiles or nations (*ethnē*) – does not appear at all. Further, nowhere in John do we get the kind of explicit attention

[17] See further Peter J. Tomson, '"Jews" in the Gospel of John as Compared with the Palestinian Talmud, the Synoptics, and Some New Testament Apocrypha', in *Anti-Judaism and the Fourth Gospel*, ed. R. Bieringer, D. Pollefeyt and F. Vandecasteele-Vanneuville (Louisville, Ky.: Westminster John Knox Press, 2001), 211–12.

to Gentiles, together with issues concerning their place in Jesus' ministry and in the life of the Church, that we have seen in Matthew and Luke–Acts. The only characters in the narrative who can be explicitly identified as Gentile are Pilate, Caesar (referred to in 19.15) and the soldiers who take part in Jesus' trial and crucifixion. Despite John's use of 'the Jews', almost all of those who follow Jesus, believe in him and thus become part of 'his own' (13.1) are themselves Jews. The only exceptions are the Samaritans, many of whom also believed in him (4.39–42).

If this were the whole picture, one might be able to argue that John's Gospel was written for a group that was still ethnically Jewish (or Jewish, with some Samaritans as well), so that even if its polemic against other Jews is harsh and fierce, it could not be described as anti-Judaic, let alone antisemitic. The whole picture, however, is not so simple.

For one thing, John seems to go out of his way to explain things that would be obvious to Jews. No Jew would need to be told, for example, that there was animosity between Jews and Samaritans (4.9), or that Passover was a 'festival of the Jews' (6.4; also 7.2). His translations of Hebrew words (1.38, 41, 42; 9.7; 20.16) might point in the same direction. For another, the scope of Jesus' saving ministry seems to be universal. Jesus is 'the true light which enlightens everyone' (1.9) or 'the Lamb of God who takes away the sin of the world' (1.29) or the one who, when lifted up, 'will draw all people' to himself (12.32). All of this is rooted in the fact that 'God loved the world' (3.16).

In addition, on two occasions we encounter references to 'Greeks' who seem to stand within the scope of Jesus' ministry. The first is found in 7.35, where, puzzled by Jesus' statement about going to a place where they will not be able to find him, 'the Jews' ask: 'Does he intend to go to the Dispersion among the Greeks [literally: the diaspora of Greeks] and teach the Greeks?' (NRSV). The second appears during Jesus' final week in Jerusalem. Among those who had come to Jerusalem for the Passover were 'some Greeks', who express a desire to see Jesus (12.20–21). Adding significance to the scene is that, upon being told that these Greeks were looking for him, Jesus for the first time declares that his 'hour' has come (12.23; cf. 2.4: 'my hour has not yet come'; also 7.30; 8.20). If Gentiles are in view here, it might suggest that John intends a contrast between Jewish opposition (see

v. 19) and Gentile belief. On the other hand, some have argued that in both cases these are Greek-speaking Jews rather than Gentiles.[18] This is not the most natural way to understand the term, however, which leads most interpreters to believe that non-Jews are in view. Even so, it is to be noted that in both passages these Gentiles are not set over against Israel or the Jews. In chapter 12, these Greeks had come to Jerusalem for the Passover, which indicates that they already had an interest in the God of Israel. Likewise, the Greeks in chapter 7 are ones who would be reached through the Jewish diaspora. If these passages provide evidence that Gentiles are included within Jesus' saving ministry for John, they are somehow linked with, rather than set in contrast to, the people of Israel.

This brings us to two further instances where John speaks of a group that stands alongside those who are the primary beneficiaries of Jesus' ministry. In chapter 10, Jesus describes himself as the 'good shepherd' (10.11), in contrast to others (presumably the Pharisees; see 9.40) who are not true shepherds of the flock. But then he goes on to speak also of 'other sheep that do not belong to this fold', whom he must gather as well (10.16). Analogously, in chapter 11, after the high priest has spoken with unwitting irony about one person dying for the people or the nation, John adds that Jesus was indeed going 'to die for the nation, and not for the nation only, but to gather into one the dispersed children of God' (11.50–52). In these instances a stronger argument might be made for seeing this second group as consisting of diaspora Jews rather than Gentiles; the contrast between 'the nation' (Judea) and the 'children of God' who have been 'dispersed' readily lends itself to such an interpretation.[19] Nevertheless, especially in view of John's interest in the salvation of 'the world' through Jesus (3.16–17), it is not surprising that a majority of interpreters see the 'other sheep', together with the 'children of God' who are not part of the 'nation', as Gentiles.

In summary, then, while John does not explicitly set 'the Jews' over against 'the Gentiles', it seems clear that Gentiles are included in the

[18] John A. T. Robinson, *Twelve New Testament Studies* (Naperville, Ill.: Allenson, 1962), 112.

[19] See especially John A. Dennis, *Jesus' Death and the Gathering of True Israel: The Johannine Appropriation of Restoration Theology in the Light of John 11.47–52*, WUNT 2/217 (Tübingen: Mohr Siebeck, 2006).

mission of Jesus. But there are differing indications as to the terms of their inclusion. On the one hand, such Gentiles are already linked with Jews and Israel, or are added to a group of believers who are drawn from Israel. On the other, to the extent that they are part of 'the world', such intermediate links perhaps fall away, so that they can be seen as the direct object of Jesus' mission.

The world

This brings us to the place of 'the world' in John's Gospel and the way in which John positions Jesus and his followers with respect to 'the world'. The question is significant not only because, when used positively (e.g. 1.29; 3.16) the term suggests that Gentiles are included within Jesus' saving ministry, but also in view of the strikingly negative use of the term, as John uses it to denote a sphere hostile to Jesus and under demonic rule, a sphere to which 'the Jews' characteristically belong. John's portrayal of 'the world', then, with its puzzling combination of positive and negative features and its relationship to 'the Jews', is important for any assessment of self-definition in the Gospel.

The ambiguous character of 'the world' is apparent in John's first reference to it (1.9–10). 'The world came into being through' the Word, who was coming into the world as its light; 'yet the world did not know him'. On the one hand, 'the world' was created by God through the Word; and so John can speak of the relationship between the Father and the Son 'before the foundation of the world' (17.24; also 17.5). On the other hand, the world was alienated from him. Positive references to 'the world', then, are not unqualifiedly positive; they have to do with God's love for a world in need of saving (3.16–17) and with Jesus as the one who 'comes into the world' in order to save it. And so we read of Jesus as 'the saviour of the world' (4.42) or the one who 'came . . . to save' it (12.47), as the light of the world (8.12; 9.5; 12.46), as the Lamb who 'takes away the sin of the world' (1.29), as the bread who 'gives life to the world' (6.33; cf. 6.51), and so on.

Apart from Jesus' presence, 'the world' is a place of evil works (7.7) and of darkness (12.46), and as such it is under condemnation (8.26; 9.39; 12.31; 16.11). It is also under the sway of one described as 'the ruler of this world' (12.31; 14.30; 16.11). Since 'the world' is incapable of recognizing or receiving 'the Spirit of truth' (14.17), presumably 'the ruler of this world' is to be identified with the devil ('the father of lies'; 8.44), though the two terms are not explicitly linked. Because Jesus (as the light of the world) exposed the deeds of those who lived in darkness, the world 'hated' him (3.19–20; 7.7; 15.18). Such hatred is also said to be due to the fact that Jesus does 'not belong to the world' (17.14, 16). This separation of Jesus from the world is not simply moral; it also has a cosmic dimension. Jesus is 'not of this world' not simply because, unlike the world, he did what was 'pleasing to' God but, more fundamentally, because he was 'from above', not 'from below' (8.23, 29). Thus, just as it was necessary for him to 'come into the world' (1.9; 3.19; 6.14; 9.39; 11.27; 16.28; 18.37), so when he has accomplished what he has been sent into the world to do (10.36; 17.18), he will 'depart from this world and go to the Father' (13.1; also 16.28; 17.11).

The relationship between Jesus and the world is also determinative for his disciples, 'those whom [God] gave [him] from the world' (17.6). Like him, they do not belong to the world (15.19); for this reason, they too will be hated by the world (15.19; 17.14, 16). Yet they too will be sent 'into the world' (17.18) and they will declare the 'word' about Jesus so that 'the world may believe' (17.20–21). While eventually Jesus will 'come again and take' them to the Father, in the meantime it is necessary for them to remain in the world (17.11, 15).

What, then, of the Jews and the world? We have already noted the way in which they are aligned at the extreme negative end: 'You are from below, I am from above; you are of this world, I am not of this world' (8.33). This, however, is not the only point of contact. Several statements in John's Gospel suggest that there is also a connection between the Jews and 'the world' seen more positively as the focus of Jesus' saving activity. In 7.4 Jesus' brothers rebuke him for doing his works 'in secret' and encourage him to go to Judea so that he can 'show [him]self to the world'. The assumption is that precisely by attending the festival of Booths and showing himself in Jerusalem he will be showing himself 'to the world'. Lest we think that this is just a mistaken notion (after all, 'not even his brothers believed in him'; 7.5), Jesus himself makes a similar statement later, in the context of his trial. In response to questioning from the high priest, Jesus says: 'I have spoken openly to the world; I have always taught in synagogues and in the temple, where all the Jews come together. I have said nothing in secret' (18.20 NRSV). By teaching in synagogue and Temple, Jesus was speaking 'to the world'. Further, since in 12.19–21 the statement 'Look, the world has gone after him' is followed immediately by the reference to the Greeks who 'wish to see Jesus', we may have an explicit illustration of how Jesus has spoken 'openly to the world' precisely by means of his ministry in the Temple. In view of this material, then, we are probably justified in seeing a link between two statements made by John the Baptist in chapter 1. After identifying Jesus as 'the Lamb of God who takes away the sin of the world' (1.29), John goes on to say that the reason he came 'baptizing with water' was so that Jesus 'might be revealed to Israel' (1.31). Somehow it is the revelation of Jesus to Israel that will enable him to take away the sin of the world.

There is thus a kind of linked parallelism in John between 'the Jews' or 'Israel' on one side and 'the world' on the other, a parallelism linked not only at the negative end but at the more positive end as well. Actually, we do not need to read as far as the account of John the Baptist; this linked parallelism probably is present in the parallelism between 1.10 and 11: 'He was in the world and the world came into being through him; yet the world did not know him. He came to his own, and his own people did not accept him.' In a recent study, Kierspel has pointed out an interesting feature of this linked parallelism.[20] While 'the Jews' and 'the world' are depicted in parallel ways in the Fourth Gospel, there is a striking distinction in attribution. Most of the occurrences of 'the world' appear on the lips of Jesus (64 of 78), especially in his Farewell Discourse (chs 13—17; some 40 occurrences). Most of the occurrences of 'the Jews' appear as words of the narrator in the narrative sections (59 of 71). Kierspel argues that this has the effect of softening the anti-Jewish effect of the Gospel. In John, 'the Jews' function as a microcosm of the whole world, for better as well as for worse. 'Right from the start, the reader knows that disbelief is a universal phenomenon and not the stigma of one particular group.'[21] As Kierspel recognizes, however, the link between 'the Jews' and 'the world' could be interpreted

[20] Lars Kierspel, *The Jews and the World in the Fourth Gospel: Parallelism, Function, and Context*, WUNT 2/220 (Tübingen: Mohr Siebeck, 2006).

[21] Ibid., 122.

in the opposite way, with the result that the anti-Jewish effect would be 'heightened' rather than 'diluted'.[22] The strength of his argument, however, has to do with the fact that the link is made at the positive end of the spectrum as well as the negative. If John's portrayal of 'the Jews' is universalized in positive ways as well as negative, it is a little harder to see such generalization as a form of demonization. Still, one could argue against this that many of the positive statements about 'the world' find no Jewish counterpart. Nowhere do we read, for example, that 'God so loved the Jews' (cf. 3.16) or that Jesus came 'not to judge the Jews but to save the Jews' (cf. 12.47).

Before looking further at the range of 'heightened' or 'diluted' interpretations, however, we need to look at one final group.

Jesus and those who believe in him

We have been looking at 'the Jews', the Gentiles and 'the world' for what they can tell us about self-definition in John – how John perceives and characterizes the ongoing community of those who believe in Jesus, especially in their relationship to the Israel of old and to the Jewish community of the present. To complete the picture, we need to look at this group directly.

John's Gospel clearly expects that the community of disciples who have gathered around Jesus during his earthly ministry will become the nucleus of an ongoing community after his death and resurrection. Jesus' death will be a means of 'gather[ing] into one the dispersed children of God' (11.52) and of 'draw[ing] all people to [him]self' (12.32). Jesus himself prays for those who will believe in him through the word of his disciples (17.20) and pronounces a benediction on 'those who have not seen and yet have come to believe' (20.29). This community will be taught and guided by the Spirit, who will come only after Jesus' resurrection and who will continue the work that Jesus has begun (14.16–17, 26; 15.26; 16.12–15).

John uses a number of terms to refer to this group. Not surprisingly, members of the group can be referred to as 'disciples', not only during Jesus' earthly ministry and with reference to specific individuals, but after his resurrection (2.22; 12.16) and in more

[22] Ibid., 112.

general terms (8.31–32; 13.35; 15.8). One of the marks of discipleship is belief (2.22; 8.31), a term that is also used to refer to the community after Jesus' resurrection (7.39; 14.12; 17.20; 20.29, 31) and to characterize the community in general (1.7, 12; 3.15–18, 36; 6.40, 47; 10.26; 11.25; 17.21; 19.35; 20.31). Other characteristic items of John's vocabulary are also used to refer to the community of believers. Those who believe thereby become children of 'light' (12.36; also 1.7–9; 3.21; 8.12; 11.9–10; 12.46); those who respond to Jesus' testimony belong to the 'truth' (18.37; also 3.21; 14.6, 17; 16.13; 17.17, 19); all who believe in Jesus will have 'eternal life' (3.15–16; also 3.36; 5.24; 6.27, 40, 47, 54; 10.10, 28; 17.2–3; 20.31). One might mention in addition several other corporate designations that appear less frequently: 'children of God' (1.12; 11.52); Jesus' 'own' (13.1; cf. 1.11); his 'friends' (15.14–15); those whom God had given to him (17.6, 9).

Of particular significance are several community appellations that seem to echo various scriptural descriptions of Israel. Followers of Jesus are described as his 'sheep' (10.16, 27; 21.15–17), with Jesus as their 'shepherd' (10.2, 11–16) – a description that resonates especially with Ezekiel 34, with its recitation of God's lengthy discourse concerning 'my sheep', the house of Israel (also Jer. 23.1–2; Mic. 2.12; 7.14; Zech. 9.16; 10.2). Similarly, John presents the disciples as branches that abide in Jesus, the 'true vine' (15.1–8) – an image that is often used of Israel itself (Ps. 80.8–16; Isa. 5.1–7; 27.2–6; Jer. 2.21). Also to be included here is the reference to the 'dispersed children of God' who will be gathered as a result of Jesus' death (11.52). While it is possible that this refers to Gentiles (in contrast to 'the nation' in v. 51), the language is evocative of the Jewish diaspora.

What, then, of the relationship between Jesus' 'own' and the people of Israel, past and present? By this point we should not be surprised that the evidence points in divergent directions. On the one hand, Jesus and his mission are presented in traditional Jewish terms, with the result that the community who believe in him could be seen as the messianic remnant of Israel,[23] who have begun to experience the restoration that was promised to Israel as a whole. The purpose of

[23] So Dennis, *Jesus' Death and the Gathering of True Israel*, 298–9.

the book is that readers 'may believe that Jesus is the Christ' (20.31), a term that John (alone of the evangelists) equates with 'Messiah' (1.41; 4.25). Jesus is the true shepherd of the flock (10.1–16), the one who dies to save not only 'the nation' but also the 'dispersed children of God' (11.52–53). If non-Jews are included within the sphere of his saving ministry, it is because 'salvation is of the Jews' (4.22) or because they are added to a Jewish 'flock' (10.16) or because they are supplemental beneficiaries of Jesus' death for 'the nation' (11.53) or because they are already associated in some way with the people of Israel (7.35; 12.20–21). Jesus' ministry to 'the world' is carried out by means of his activity in synagogues and the Temple (18.20; also 1.29, 31; 7.4).

On the other hand, however, if John wants to present Jesus' 'sheep' as the restored and renewed remnant of the flock of Israel, the 'renewal' seems to be so far-reaching that the remnant is scarcely recognizable in comparison with the original flock. Yes, John wants his readers to believe that Jesus is the Messiah (20.31). But this Messiah is also the Son of God (20.31), and while 'Son of God' appears as a messianic term in Qumran literature (*4QFlorilegium*; *4QAramaic Apocalypse*; cf. 2 Sam. 7.14; Ps. 2.7), Jesus as Son of God in John's Gospel is so explicitly divine in nature as to be far above and beyond any concept of the Messiah that can be found in first-century Judaism. It is not surprising that 'the Jews' want to stone Jesus for blasphemy, in that, 'though only a human being, [he is] making [him]self God' (10.33 NRSV). Yes, Jesus is linked with constituent elements of Israel's identity: the Passover lamb (1.29, 36); the Temple (2.19–22); manna (6.32–65); the sheep (10.1–16); the vine (15.1–8); and so on. But the link is so overpowering that the original significance of these identity markers seems to be swallowed up in a pattern of spiritualization that leaves little in the way of common ground between the old flock and the new remnant. Given this relationship between Christ and the defining marks of Israel, it is not surprising that 'the Jews had already agreed that anyone who confessed him to be the Christ would be put out of the synagogue' (9.22). The idea that belief in Jesus would result in expulsion from the synagogue (found also in 12.42 and 16.2) needs to be seen in conjunction with the existence of what might be called synagogue believers – people who believe in Jesus but in a manner that allows them to remain in the synagogue (12.42–43; 19.38). While John accounts for this simply on the basis of fear (also 7.13), it suggests instead that his conception of Jesus as 'Christ and Son of God' was such a drastic revision of traditional Jewish conceptions that, unlike some other Jewish believers, John and his community could no longer remain within the Jewish fold.

The problem posed by Christian self-definition in John's Gospel, then, can be summarized as follows. On the one hand, if we bracket out John's use of 'the Jews' and other unique aspects of his theological outlook, we get a picture not unlike what we have seen in Luke–Acts or in Matthew. Jesus' mission was primarily to Israel, to whom he presented himself as Messiah and Son of God. His ministry produced a division among the people of Israel, with the religious leaders taking the lead in opposing him and at least a considerable minority of the common people believing in him. Those who believe in him can be seen as true Israelites and the remnant of Israel. While Jesus' ministry is also significant for non-Jews, it is only through Israel that the Gentiles are included. At the sub-stratum of John's Gospel, then, is a story of Jesus and his followers that stands in substantial continuity with the story of Israel.

On the other hand, however, this story is overlaid with a distinctive theological construction in which the opponents of Jesus are referred to simply as 'the Jews', a group aligned with 'the world' and its ruler the devil, and in which the characteristic elements of Israel's identity and messianic hope are so redefined by John's distinctive christology that any continuity between the Israel of old and John's community of Christ-believers may well seem to have been severed.

In the interpretation of John, some see the theological overlay as decisive, and thus judge the overall force of John's Gospel to be anti-Jewish and, at least potentially, antisemitic.[24] Others attempt to limit the definition of 'the Jews', seeing it as referring only to the

---

[24] Culpepper (R. Alan Culpepper, 'Anti-Judaism in the Fourth Gospel as a Theological Problem for Christian Interpreters', in *Anti-Judaism and the Fourth Gospel*, ed. R. Bieringer, D. Pollefeyt and F. Vandecasteele-Vanneuville (Louisville, Ky.: Westminster John Knox Press, 2001), 61–82) and Smiga (George M. Smiga, *Pain and Polemic: Anti-Judaism in the Gospels* (New York: Paulist Press, 1992), 134–73) are examples of those who tend in this direction, though not without nuance and qualification.

Jewish leaders[25] or to residents in Judea,[26] or some combination of the two,[27] and thus to open up the possibility of a more continuous reading of John's story. Still others argue that for John 'the Jews' simply represent a microcosm of 'the world',[28] so that John's story is one in which the distinction between Jew and Gentile is ultimately transcended in a larger universal sphere of interest.

Choosing among these various interpretations of John is no easy matter. John's story of Jesus was written in a particular time and place, however, which means that there is another dimension to be considered.

Social location of John and his intended readers

Up until the middle of the twentieth century, it was common among scholarly interpreters to understand John as dependent on the other Gospels and written for a Church that was predominantly Gentile in composition and outlook. This interpretation was based partly on John's polemical use of 'the Jews', which seemed to imply a non-Jewish viewpoint, and partly on his dualistic language (e.g. light/darkness, truth/lie, above/below), which many believed to be a sure indicator of Gentile origins. This consensus was brought to an end by the discovery of the Dead Sea Scrolls. The scrolls opened a window onto a first-century Jewish group that was completely separated from the Gentile world and yet used similar dualistic language in its self-description (e.g. 'sons of light' and 'sons of darkness'). This led scholars to take another look at aspects of John's Gospel that have already caught our attention – for example, the almost complete absence of Gentiles, or the preoccupation with Jewish festivals and concerns. This led in turn to a thoroughgoing reassessment of John's

---

[25] E.g. David Rensberger, 'Anti-Judaism and the Gospel of John', in *Anti-Judaism and the Gospels*, ed. William R. Farmer (Harrisburg, Pa.: Trinity Press International, 1999), 125.

[26] Malcolm F. Lowe, 'Who Were the Ioudaioi?' *Novum Testamentum* 18 (1976): 101–30.

[27] E.g. Dennis, *Jesus' Death and the Gathering of True Israel*, 4, 254–5; Stephen Motyer, 'The Fourth Gospel and the Salvation of Israel: An Appeal for a New Start', in *Anti-Judaism and the Fourth Gospel*, ed. R. Bieringer, D. Pollefeyt and F. Vandecasteele-Vanneuville (Louisville, Ky.: Westminster John Knox Press, 2001), 83–100.

[28] Kierspel, *The Jews and the World*.

relationship with the Jewish world and to the emergence of a new consensus.

A leading figure in this new consensus was Raymond Brown, whose work[29] can be used to represent a much larger set of scholars and studies. These studies are based on the assumption that the Gospel provides us with a window into the nature and character of the group to which it was originally addressed. This assumption is worked out with reference to two aspects of John's Gospel. One has to do with a set of apparent seams and discontinuities in the narrative; these we will consider a little later. The other, which we will look at first, concerns the texture of the narrative itself. In writing his Gospel (it is believed), John has inscribed the experiences and struggles of his own particular Christian group onto the story of Jesus, producing a narrative that can be read at two levels. A careful reading of the first level – the story of Jesus itself – can reveal, at a second level, something of the historical situation and social location of John's community.

Such a two-level reading pays particular attention to material we have already considered – Christian self-understanding as defined with respect to 'the Jews', Israel, Gentiles, 'the world', synagogue believers, and so on. Several other elements are also important. One is the figure whom John describes as 'the disciple whom Jesus loved' (13.21–30; 19.25–27; 20.1–10; 21.4–8, 20–25). Not only does this description serve to set him apart from the other disciples, but this disciple usually appears alongside Peter, who suffers from the implied comparison in that the Beloved Disciple is portrayed as closer to Jesus, more spiritually perceptive, more faithful and so on. The final reference to the Beloved Disciple identifies him as 'the one who is testifying to these things and who has written them' (21.24) – that is, as the author of the Gospel. It is also observed that the Twelve do not play a major role in John's Gospel and, where they do appear, it is with negative overtones (6.70–71; 20.24–25).

Related to this is the prominence of Jerusalem and Judea. In the Synoptics, Jesus is in Judea only once during his ministry – the week leading up to his crucifixion. In John, however, he is found in Judea

---

[29] See especially Raymond E. Brown, *The Gospel According to John*, 2 vols, Anchor Bible (Garden City, NY: Doubleday, 1966 and 1970); *The Community of the Beloved Disciple* (New York: Paulist Press, 1979).

as often as in Galilee (1.29–42; 2.13—4.3; 5.1–47; 7.1—20.31). Perhaps not coincidentally, the Beloved Disciple is found primarily in Judea (chapter 21 is the only exception).

Another element that is used in a two-level reading of John is the emphasis on John the Baptist. All four Gospels see John the Baptist as important but in a subordinate way, presenting him as a forerunner whose role was simply to prepare the way for Jesus himself. In the Fourth Gospel, however, this theme is especially pronounced. John the Baptist is mentioned even in the prologue (1.6–8, 15). In his first appearance, he goes out of the way to deny that he is the Messiah (1.19–28). When he first encounters Jesus, he identifies him as 'the Lamb of God who takes away the sin of the world' and steers two of his disciples in Jesus' direction (1.29–36). In 3.31–36, John the Baptist even speaks of Jesus in the elevated language characteristic of Jesus' own discourses (e.g. 'The one who comes from above is above all'; 'The Father loves the Son and has placed all things in his hands. Whoever believes in the Son has eternal life' NRSV).

Finally, a little more needs to be said about an element that we have touched on already – the idea that any who believed in Jesus 'would be put out of the synagogue'. In 9.22 this appears in categorical terms: 'the Jews had already agreed that anyone who confessed Jesus to be the Messiah would be put out of the synagogue' (NRSV). On several occasions we find references to people who hid their belief 'for fear that they would be put out of the synagogue' (12.42–43 NRSV; also 19.38). The other side of the coin is represented by those believers who confess their faith in Christ openly, and are thus forced out of the synagogue. There is one such instance in John: the healed blind man in chapter 9, who believes in Jesus and thus is driven out (9.34–38). Jesus warns that there will be more in the future (16.2). Many interpreters find these references to be anachronistic. It is hard to imagine that during Jesus' earthly ministry someone would have been forced out of the synagogue simply for believing that Jesus was the Messiah. There is certainly no evidence of this in any of the other Gospels. At a later time, however, this could well have been the experience of Christians, especially those whose understanding of Jesus was as elevated as that found in the Fourth Gospel. Louis Martyn, one of the earliest proponents of a two-level reading of John, has argued that this should be understood with reference to the *birkath ha-minim*, the insertion into the daily synagogue prayers (the Eighteen

Benedictions) of a malediction against the *minim*, which he took to be a reference to Christians.[30]

Before exploring the significance of this for a two-level reading of John, we need to look at a second aspect of the Gospel. John's narrative is marked by a number of puzzling seams or discontinuities. In 3.22, for example, Jesus and his disciples are said to come into the land of Judea. But from 2.13 and all through chapter 3 he is already there. In 6.1 it is said that 'Jesus went to the other side of the sea of Galilee', which seems to imply that before this point he was on 'this side' of the sea of Galilee. But right to the end of chapter 5 Jesus is in Jerusalem, several days' journey to the south. At 14.31, after he has been speaking to his disciples at the last supper for quite a while, Jesus says to them: 'Rise, let us be on our way'. But what follows is three more chapters of discourse, before they finally leave and go on their way (18.1).

The most striking seam has to do with the final chapter. At the end of chapter 20, we are presented with a ringing statement of purpose that seems to bring the Gospel to a grand conclusion: 'Now Jesus did many other signs in the presence of his disciples, which are not written in this book. But these are written so that you may come to believe that Jesus is the Messiah, the Son of God, and that through believing you may have life in his name' (20.30–31). A first-time reader would be surprised, then, to discover that the Gospel continues with a whole additional chapter, a central feature of which is the relationship between the Beloved Disciple and Peter. At the end of this chapter the Beloved Disciple is identified as the author, though not without some ambiguity. The statement is made on behalf of a group who are obviously distinct from the Beloved Disciple ('we know that his testimony is true'), which means that these verses at least (vv. 24–25) could not have been written by him. Further, since the preceding verses seem to imply that the Beloved Disciple has died (otherwise, why try to dispel the rumour that he would not die before Jesus' coming?), it is reasonable to conclude that the whole chapter was written after his death.

While various theories have been proposed to account for these observations, the most compelling has been the suggestion that

[30] J. Louis Martyn, *History and Theology in the Fourth Gospel* (New York: Harper & Row, 1968). Earlier, Baum had made a similar suggestion; see the discussion at the start of this chapter.

the Gospel was written in several stages, the final one of which took place after the death of the Beloved Disciple. While this disciple had a leading role in the writing of the main part of the Gospel, the whole of chapter 21, together with other portions of the Gospel (e.g. chs 15—17), was added after his death.

Putting these two sets of observations together, Brown and others have argued for a reconstruction of the history of John's community and the formation of the Gospel that can be sketched out as follows. This community is rooted in a Judean group of Jesus' disciples, some of whom may have initially been followers of John the Baptist and one of whom was the person referred to in the Gospel as 'the disciple whom Jesus loved'. While this disciple might have been John, one of the Twelve, it is more probable that he was native to Judea, not Galilee, and thus represented a different group of Jesus' followers. In the post-Easter period this community developed under the leadership of this disciple into a group distinct from other circles of churches, especially those associated with Peter. Perhaps at an early stage of its history, this group incorporated a number of converts from the Samaritans. Under the leadership of the Beloved Disciple, this group developed the distinctive theological outlook, themes and style that we find later in the Gospel, especially in the discourses. During this period, a first edition of the Gospel began to take shape. Probably because of the character of its distinctive theology, especially its elevated Christology, this group came into fierce conflict with its Jewish neighbours, particularly the synagogue leadership. This conflict resulted in the expulsion of the community from the synagogue. At some point, perhaps after the war with Rome, the community may have left Judea entirely, settling in the diaspora (later tradition associates John's Gospel with Ephesus). After the death of the Beloved Disciple, his followers expanded the Gospel, adding the epilogue (ch. 21) and some additional material (e.g. chs 15—17).

While such a reconstruction does not resolve the problems posed by John's depiction of 'the Jews' and related aspects, it does put them into a context in which they might be more fully understood. The Gospel was written by a community of Jewish Christ-believers who had experienced a painful expulsion from the synagogue. Because of this, together with a relocation to the diaspora, they began to refer to the opponents of Jesus and the disciples simply as 'the Judeans' or 'the Jews'. This usage was incorporated into the Gospel during the later stages of its formation, resulting in the odd features of the usage that we have observed.

To be sure, such reconstructions have not gone uncriticized. Many have objected to Martyn's appeal to the *birkath ha-minim* benediction, arguing that the evidence does not suggest any widespread initiative directed specifically against Jewish Christians and leading to their expulsion. This objection is not fatal to the reconstruction, however, since all that is required is a local conflict involving a specific community of Christ-believers, not a generalized expulsion. But in addition, Reinhartz has demonstrated that a two-level reading of other sections of the Gospel (e.g. ch. 11) would produce quite a different picture of the relationship between John's community and 'the Jews'.[31] Further, Bauckham and others have mounted a strong offensive against the idea that the Gospels, John included, were written for distinct localized communities, arguing instead that they were addressed to a wider, more general Christian readership.[32]

Still, the dominant interpretation of John's Gospel is that it has emerged out of a fierce, localized conflict between a particular community of Jewish Christians and the Jewish synagogue. Even so, however, one's assessment of John's depiction of 'the Jews' and their characteristics will depend on whether one sees John's community as still attempting to remain within the boundaries of the wider Jewish world, or as now completely separated from it and directing its attention to the Gentile world.[33] This brings us to the question of the Gospel's purpose with respect to its intended readers.

---

31 Adele Reinhartz, '"Jews" and Jews in the Fourth Gospel', in *Anti-Judaism and the Fourth Gospel*, ed. R. Bieringer, D. Pollefeyt and F. Vandecasteele-Vanneuville (Louisville, Ky.: Westminster John Knox Press, 2001), 223–4.

32 Richard Bauckham (ed.), *The Gospels for All Christians: Rethinking the Gospel Audiences* (Grand Rapids: Eerdmans, 1998); *The Testimony of the Beloved Disciple: Narrative, History, and Theology in the Gospel of John* (Grand Rapids: Baker Academic, 2007).

33 For the former, see e.g. Motyer, 'The Fourth Gospel and the Salvation of Israel'; Dennis, *Jesus' Death and the Gathering of True Israel*, 296–311. For the latter, see e.g. John Townsend, 'The Gospel of John and the Jews: The Story of a Religious Divorce', in *Antisemitism and the Foundations of Christianity*, ed. Alan T. Davies (New York and Toronto: Paulist Press, 1979), 83–4; Culpepper, 'Anti-Judaism in the Fourth Gospel as a Theological Problem for Christian Interpreters'; Kierspel, *The Jews and the World*, 181–213.

Rhetorical function of John's treatment of Jews and Judaism

As we have seen, John's Gospel includes an explicit statement of purpose (20.30–31), which makes it very clear that the Gospel was intended as an instrument of persuasion. John wants his readers to believe 'that Jesus is the Messiah, the Son of God, and that through believing you may have life in his name' (NRSV). There is no more that needs to be said here about the content of this belief. But who are the intended readers ('so that *you* may believe')? And how does the Gospel's treatment of Jews and Judaism fit into this intended purpose?

The transmission of John's Gospel has added to the complexity of this question, in that some early manuscripts are worded in such a way as to suggest that the Gospel was written to those who already believed, while other, equally reliable manuscripts suggest a readership of potential believers. The difference has to do with different forms of the verb 'believe' (20.31), forms that differ by a single letter. The word in the first group of manuscripts can be rendered 'so that you may continue to believe' (*pisteuēte*); in the others it could have the sense 'so that you may come to believe' (*pisteusēte*). If John's Gospel does indeed reflect the actual experience of a community of believers, the first reading is probably to be preferred; the purpose of the Gospel was to affirm and strengthen a community of readers who already had come to belief. Even so, however, a concern for potential believers cannot be excluded. As we have seen, John expects that others will come to belief precisely through the word of those who already were believers (17.20; see also 20.29). Still, a question of emphasis remains. Was the Gospel intended primarily for internal consumption, to strengthen and reassure a community of believers? If so, John's treatment of 'the Jews' and Judaism serves primarily to reaffirm the identity and self-conception of the community, by underscoring the differences between them and 'the Jews'. Or was the Gospel intended to assist with the task of 'gather[ing] into one the dispersed children of God' (11.52) and of 'draw[ing] all people to [Jesus]' (12.32–33)? If so, was this mission directed primarily at Jews, or had it become primarily a mission to Gentiles?

As we have seen, some interpreters believe that a complete separation between John's community and the world of Judaism has taken place, so that any mission carried out by the community was directed at the Gentile world. If so, it would be hard to avoid the conclusion that potential non-Jewish converts would have received the message that by coming to belief in Jesus they would also be expected to adopt a negative attitude towards the Jewish people per se. Even if the polemical use of 'the Jews' developed in the context of a bitter dispute between groups, both of which were Jewish, the term would inevitably have taken on an ethnic – and thus potentially antisemitic – meaning in the context of a Gentile mission.

Others, however, argue that the mission was directed primarily at Jews, in a context after the war with Rome when the Temple was destroyed and the traditional structures of Judaism were in disarray. In such a context, John's community declared Jesus to be the Messiah of Israel and the replacement for the destroyed Temple, presented itself as the representatives of 'the nation' for whom the Messiah had died (11.51), and invited other Israelites[34] – perhaps especially those of the diaspora (cf. 11.52)[35] – to join them. In order to bring these Israelites to belief in Jesus, John's community had to dissuade them from giving their allegiance to those others, found especially among the synagogue leadership in Judea (i.e. 'the Jews'), who were also attempting to rebuild the house of Israel after the war with Rome. In such a situation, John's treatment of 'the Jews' and Judaism would have functioned as an instrument of persuasion in an inner-Jewish debate. While John's choice of instrument might have been regrettable, especially in light of subsequent history, it should not – in this reading of things – be seen as essentially anti-Jewish.

Of course, if the mission was not directed exclusively at Jews but also included Gentiles ('all people'; 12.32), John's persuasive strategy takes on an ethnically anti-Jewish dimension that would increase in proportion to the success of the mission.

---

[34] James D. G. Dunn, 'An Embarrassment of History: Reflections on the Problem of "Anti-Judaism" in the Fourth Gospel', in *Anti-Judaism and the Fourth Gospel*, ed. R. Bieringer, D. Pollefeyt and F. Vandecasteele-Vanneuville (Louisville, Ky.: Westminster John Knox Press, 2001), 41–60.

[35] Motyer, 'The Fourth Gospel and the Salvation of Israel', 97–8.

Concluding observations

Is John's Gospel antisemitic? anti-Judaic? supersessionistic? As was the case with Matthew and Luke–Acts, our answer to these questions depends on where we place John on our three-dimensional grid (self-definition, social location and rhetorical function). At the end of our discussion of the first of these axes, we observed the tension between the very Jewish story that lies at the base of the Gospel, and the distinctive theological-polemical overlay that sets John apart from the other Gospels. While our consideration of the other two axes has added texture and detail to this tension, the interpretive challenge remains fundamentally the same. What balance is to be struck between the Jewishness of the story and the – at least potentially – anti-Jewishness of the overlay? Again, our answer to this question will emerge from the interpretive decisions that we make about the sets of interrelated questions that confront us along each axis.

5
Paul

> God's wrath has overtaken them at last.
>
> (1 Thessalonians 2.16 NRSV)

> But what does the scripture say? 'Drive out the slave and her child; for the child of the slave will not share the inheritance with the child of the free woman.' (Galatians 4.30 NRSV)

1 Thessalonians 2.14–16 represents Paul's harshest outburst against his Jewish compatriots. In an attempt to encourage believers in Thessalonica who were experiencing persecution, he compares them to churches in Judea who had suffered at the hands of 'the Jews', whom he goes on to castigate for their sins – killing Jesus and the prophets; persecuting 'us'; hindering the mission to the Gentiles; thus 'displeasing God and opposing everyone' – and whom he declares now to be subject to 'God's wrath'. The harshness of the outburst is unusual in Paul; nowhere else, for example, does he use 'the Jews' in a polemical way. While the passage is not for this reason to be dismissed, the more serious problem presented by the 'apostle to the Gentiles', however, lies elsewhere. In his depiction of the human plight under sin and the divinely provided solution in Christ, Paul systematically associates the Jewish law with the former, aligning both the law and the people who take their identity from it with the negative side of a set of binary pairs – law/grace; law/promise; works of law/faith; curse/blessing; sin/righteousness; ministry of condemnation/ministry of justification; flesh/spirit; and, in Galatians 4.21–31, Hagar the slave woman, the mother of slaves/Sarah the free woman, the mother of the free. At the same time, however, not only does this negative treatment of the law stand alongside very positive statements, but on virtually every topic of interest to us here, Paul presents us with a puzzle of conflicting statements.

Somewhat surprisingly, perhaps, Jules Isaac's few references to Paul highlight the positive side of the puzzle. While he takes note of 1 Thessalonians 2.14–16, he reads it as a reference simply to a 'Jerusalemite clique' and denies that it represents a negative judgement on the people of Israel as a whole.[1] Elsewhere he cites Paul as a witness for Jesus' Jewishness (Rom. 1.3; 9.3–5), his life 'under the law' (Gal. 4.4) and his role as a 'servant to the circumcised' (Rom. 15.8).[2] He also notes with approval Paul's emphasis on a Jewish remnant (Rom. 11.2–5) and his declaration that God will ultimately have mercy on all (Rom. 11.32).[3]

Of course, Isaac's primary concern has to do with Jesus and the Gospels. One can get a better idea of the things to which he might have taken exception if he had set out to treat Paul more directly, by looking at the charges that Gregory Baum sets out to refute. Baum recognizes that Romans 9—11, with its interest both in a believing Jewish 'remnant' and in the ultimate salvation of 'all Israel', is often seen as an anomaly, a striking departure from the universalism that is found elsewhere in the writings of the 'apostle to the Gentiles' (e.g. 'for there is no distinction between Jew and Greek'; Rom. 10.12 NRSV). Thus he leaves this portion to the end of his discussion, dealing first with 'Israel, the Chosen People' and then with 'The Abrogation of the Law'. His purpose is to demonstrate 'that there is hardly anything in Romans 9—11 which is not also expressed' elsewhere in his epistles.[4] As he carries out this purpose, one can readily see the kinds of accusations against which he hopes to defend Paul: that Paul's new identity as the apostle to the Gentiles carried with it an abandonment of his Jewish identity; that Paul's message of a gospel of salvation for all without distinction meant that the distinction between Jew and Gentile was now irrelevant; that Israel had now lost whatever status it had as the chosen people of God; and that Paul's depiction of life under the law ('an accursed way, void of promise, a ministration of death, a state of slavery'[5]) is seriously at odds with the way in which most of his Jewish contemporaries would have described their Torah-shaped existence. In defending Paul against

[1] Jules Isaac, *Jesus and Israel* (New York: Holt, Rinehart & Winston, 1971), 236–8.

[2] Ibid., 11, 19, 387, 402.

[3] Ibid., 4, 238.

[4] Gregory Baum, *The Jews and the Gospel: A Re-Examination of the New Testament* (Westminster, Md.: Newman Press, 1961), 173.

[5] Ibid., 196.

such accusations, however, Baum presents counter-arguments that, ironically, might be seen as underscoring the problem rather than as eliminating it.

For Baum, any negative comments that Paul might make about the law and the people who adhered to it were always derived from his more fundamental belief that the age of preparation has been succeeded by the age of the Messiah, which has been ushered in through the resurrection of Christ. The law of Moses, which was the defining feature of the preparatory era, has been completely fulfilled in Christ and has now been replaced by something better and greater. To the accusation that the gospel represents the failure of God's promises to Israel, (Baum's) Paul replies: 'God breaks his promises by giving more'.[6] Further, the arrival of the messianic age has produced a schism within Israel – the Jewish-Christian remnant on one side, the unbelieving Jews on the other. Israel, then, has not been rejected; rather, it has been reduced to the believing remnant, who themselves represent the true continuation of Israel. As for the Gentile believers, they represent the fulfilment of Isaiah's expectation that Gentiles will find salvation by being added to the Israel of the end-times. Thus, '[t]he Jews who believe constitute the faithful Israel, the centre of the new community in natural continuity with the posterity of Abraham; and to this Israel of the spirit the Gentile nations are adjoined'.[7] As for the unbelieving Jews, they are clinging to 'a religion devoid of promise' and thus 'have missed their destiny'.[8] Still, Paul anticipates that this state of affairs is temporary, Jewish unbelief opening up a period of time in which the Gentiles might be brought in. When this period comes to an end, 'all Israel' will be converted to Christ and will become incorporated into the 'true Israel' that stands at the heart of the Church.

Rosemary Ruether shares with Baum the perception that Paul's negative treatment of Torah religion is rooted in a conception of an eschatological division of the ages. But in her opinion Paul has intensified this division into a sharp dualism, with the result that no positive value at all is to be attached to Torah religion and, by extension, to Israel.

---

[6] Ibid., 212; also 181, 191–5.
[7] Ibid., 242.
[8] Ibid., 252, 205.

For (Ruether's) Paul, the two ages (aeons) are not thought of as successive historical periods related in any promise-fulfilment schema. 'Paul clearly does not think of the Church as a "historical religion", which superseded Judaism in a relation of historical continuity.'[9] Instead, the two aeons are discontinuous and antithetical 'worlds' or spheres of existence, a conception that represents 'a remarkable fusion of Gnostic and apocalyptic dualisms'.[10] The earthly aeon of finite fleshly existence, ruled by demonic beings ('principalities and powers'), is set over against the heavenly aeon of spiritual existence, which has now been made accessible in Christ. In saying that the law was given 'through angels' (Gal. 3.19), by which 'Paul means those lower and inferior powers which reign over the spheres of the fallen cosmos',[11] he was clearly aligning Torah religion with life in this aeon, life under the powers of sin and death. Thus he can speak of the Torah as 'the dispensation of death', which stands in contrast to the glorious dispensation of the Spirit (2 Cor. 3.7–8). In Galatians 4.21–31, Paul uses the figures of Hagar and Sarah to symbolize these two dispensations or aeons, together with the people associated with them. Just as Hagar was not to share the inheritance of Sarah, so the people of Israel never stood in any positive relationship with God: 'Judaism for Paul is not only *not* an ongoing covenant of salvation where men continue to be related in true worship of God: it *never* was such a community of faith and grace.'[12]

To be sure, Ruether recognizes that in Romans 9—11 Paul struggles with what might be seen as the logical corollary of his position, namely, 'that historical election means nothing at all to God'.[13] But since the 'mystery' that he arrives at has to do with the ultimate conversion of the Jews to Christ, she concludes that his purpose 'is not to concede any ongoing validity to Judaism, but rather to assure the *ultimate vindication of the Church*'.[14] In short, 'Paul's position was unquestionably that of anti-Judaism.'[15]

---

[9] Rosemary R. Ruether, *Faith and Fratricide: The Theological Roots of Anti-Semitism* (Minneapolis: Seabury, 1974), 103.
[10] Ibid., 101.
[11] Ibid., 99.
[12] Ibid., 104.
[13] Ibid., 105.
[14] Ibid., 107; italics hers.
[15] Ibid., 104.

In keeping with the pattern followed in previous chapters, our exploration here will begin with a consideration of self-definition. We will focus on the seven letters for which Pauline authorship is undisputed (Romans, 1 and 2 Corinthians, Galatians, Philippians, 1 Thessalonians and Philemon), though the picture would not change dramatically if we were to include the others.

Self-definition in Paul

The 35 years since the publication of Ruether's *Faith and Fratricide* have witnessed dramatic changes in the interpretation of Paul, a shift of perspective that has put the question of 'Paul and Judaism' into a significantly different framework. Speaking in broad terms, we can describe this as a shift from a universalistic framework, one in which Jew and Gentile are seen as secondary and even peripheral categories, to one in which Jew and Gentile are seen as more central for Paul and more fundamental for our understanding of him.

In what I have called the universalistic framework, it was assumed that Paul's primary concern is with human beings in general – their plight under sin and the possibility of their salvation in Christ. The human plight primarily has to do with guilt: because of their sins and transgressions, human beings have become guilty before a God who demands righteousness, and thus have come under divine condemnation. The fundamental need, then, is a way in which sins might be forgiven and guilt removed, so that human beings might be declared righteous (justified) and condemnation might be replaced with reconciliation. This is what Christ has accomplished; in his death 'for us', he has made it possible for God to forgive the guilty and to declare them righteous. In order to benefit from what Christ has done, human beings need to recognize their status as guilty sinners, to forgo any futile attempt to establish a righteous status on their own, and to respond in faith to what God has done for them in Christ. In this reading of Paul, the law comes into the picture partly because of its ability to identify sin and thus to establish human guilt, and partly because Torah religion served as a prime example of a misguided attempt to establish a righteous status through one's own achievement and merit – that is, through 'works'. Such a pattern of universal salvation, it was thought, lay behind Paul's succinct slogan 'justification by faith (in Christ) and not by works (of the law)'.

This version of the universalistic framework, of course, is characteristic of the Reformation and subsequent Protestant tradition. But while there were significant points of disagreement between the Reformers and the Roman Catholic Church – for example, whether Paul used the verb 'to justify' (*dikaioun*) with the sense of 'to declare righteous' or 'to make righteous' – the Catholic side of the debate was no less universalistic. Indeed, this debate needs to be seen as existing within a universalistic framework that is deeply rooted in Gentile Christianity as a whole. Further, the more modern historical-critical examination of Paul emerged within this framework as well. Beginning with F. C. Baur in the first half of the nineteenth century and continuing well into the twentieth, Paul was regularly seen as the one who was able to break through the narrow bounds of Judaism and to create a universal, spiritual religion that was free of ethnic encumbrances, and so was able to flourish in the wider Gentile world.

This universalistic way of reading Paul brought with it a number of corollaries, several of which should be mentioned here. One is that Paul's depiction of Torah religion – a religion inherently incapable of dealing with sin, even as it also fostered an attitude of smug self-righteousness – was an accurate description of the Judaism of his day. A second is that Paul's Damascus experience is to be understood as a true conversion – that is, as a personal transformation in which he abandoned one religion (a religion based on works) and entered another (one based on faith). A third is that Romans 9—11, with its apparent interest in preserving some sort of special place for the people of Israel, seems to be inconsistent with Paul's more fundamental conviction that ethnic distinctions have been transcended and abolished in Christ ('there is no Jew nor Gentile'). It was often thought, then, that here Paul simply allowed some residual ethnic loyalty to override his more fundamental convictions, which means that it should not be accorded any real significance in our reconstructions of his thought.

As has been mentioned, in more recent times this universalistic framework has been challenged and, for many, has been replaced by one in which Paul's identity as a Jewish apostle to the (non-Jewish) nations is taken to be fundamental. This development has been spurred on by the same factors that have driven the discussion of 'the New Testament and anti-Judaism' more generally (as were identified in Chapter 1): the post-Holocaust search for causes; the end of Christendom and the emergence of religious pluralism; the increase of scholarly dialogue between Jews and Christians; and advances in our understanding of Second-Temple Judaism. Paul being Paul, however, this development has followed its own course.

The key point in this development was the publication in 1977 of E. P. Sanders's *Paul and Palestinian Judaism*.[16] There were important precursors, however; as Sanders himself readily acknowledged, he constructed his work on a foundation laid by a number of predecessors. One group of predecessors, containing both Jewish scholars (e.g. Claude Montefiore) and Christian scholars who were thoroughly familiar with Jewish sources (e.g. George Foot Moore), objected to Paul's depiction of Torah religion. One objection concerned Paul's statements about the law's inability to deal with sin. In Romans Paul argues that the law is unable to do anything more than simply to demonstrate that human beings have fallen short of the divine requirements and thus stand guilty before God. All the law can do is to reveal sin; it has no power to overcome it or to provide forgiveness. However, this pessimistic assessment ignores (it was argued) the fact that the Torah itself anticipates human sin and makes provision for it – through repentance, atonement (e.g. through temple sacrifice) and forgiveness. Why did Paul not mention this? And even more tellingly: if the presence of sin is enough to demonstrate the ineffectiveness of a religious system, why is it that evidence of sinfulness in Paul's own congregations (Corinth!) does not call his Christ religion into question?

A second objection had to do with Paul's doctrine of 'works' – the idea that Torah religion functioned as a means by which human beings attempted to establish a right relationship with God (i.e. righteousness) on the basis of their own meritorious achievement, and thus the idea that Torah religion was the polar opposite of a religion of grace. Such an idea, however, ignores (it was argued) the fact that the Torah is more than a set of individual commandments. Instead it is part of a covenant relationship, a relationship established by God through God's own gracious promise to Abraham. The giving of the commandments at Sinai, after all, was subsequent to the exodus from

[16] E. P. Sanders, *Paul and Palestinian Judaism* (Philadelphia: Fortress Press, 1977).

Egypt. Jewish people keep the commandments not in order to achieve a relationship with God, but as a way living within a relationship already established and thus as a joyful response to God's gracious election of Israel. No Jew with a healthy experience of the covenant would have thought that law and grace were at odds with each other.

Why, then, did Paul treat the law as a works-religion that was capable only of revealing sin and producing guilt? A common answer (e.g. Montefiore) was that because of his diaspora upbringing in Tarsus, Paul was unfamiliar with Torah religion in all its rich vitality.[17] In other words, because he was familiar only with an impoverished Hellenistic form of Judaism, he simply misunderstood Torah religion. A more suspicious answer is that Paul deliberately misrepresented Judaism in order to ensure the success of his preaching among the Gentiles.

Another possibility, however, is that Paul himself has been misrepresented or misunderstood by his interpreters. This brings us back to Sanders and to a second group of predecessors. In the early part of the twentieth century, both William Wrede and Albert Schweitzer argued forcefully that to interpret Paul by starting with his statements about 'justification by faith rather than works' and assuming that this formulation is central to his thought, is inevitably to misunderstand him.[18] They observed that for an idea that supposedly represented the heart and centre of Paul's doctrine of salvation, it played a strikingly limited role in his letters. It appears only in Galatians, Romans and a small section of Philippians and thus only in contexts where Paul is defending his Gentile mission against any suggestion that Gentiles needed to be circumcised (if they were male) and to observe the whole law in order to be full and legitimate members of the Church. Elsewhere it is absent, which means that Paul can deal with all sorts of problem situations and develop all sorts of theological discourses without feeling any need to refer back to the supposedly foundational doctrine of 'justification by faith not works'. In particular, while Paul is evidently concerned that his converts no longer live in sin but 'walk in newness of life' (Rom. 6.1–4), he makes no

[17] C. G. Montefiore, *Judaism and St. Paul: Two Essays* (London: Max Goschen, 1914).

[18] William Wrede, *Paul* (London: Green, 1907); Albert Schweitzer, *The Mysticism of Paul the Apostle* (London: A&C Black, 1931).

attempt to construct his ethics on the foundation of justification by faith. Instead, he typically begins with a believer's union with Christ ('we have died with Christ'; Rom. 6.8). Conversely, when he turns to ethical matters, he can urge his converts to 'do' all sorts of things – to celebrate the Lord's supper properly, to care for the poor, to support their teachers, to abstain from sexual immorality and other forms of wrongdoing, and so on – without adding any warning about the dangers of 'works righteousness'. Even in Galatians, when dealing with ethical instruction, he urges his readers not to 'grow weary in doing what is right' and even to 'boast' in 'their own work' (Gal. 6.9, 4)! In other words, the only kind of 'works' to which Paul objects are those things that would turn Gentiles into Jews (circumcision, observance of food laws and so on). In fact, said Wrede and Schweitzer, this is how we are to understand Paul's faith–works doctrine. 'Justification by faith not works' is Paul's abbreviation of a line of argument that he developed for the specific purposes of defending the idea that Gentiles are to be included in the Church (i.e. considered righteous) without having to become converts to Judaism in the process (i.e. to perform those 'works' that would turn them into Jews).

Building on the work of these and other predecessors, Sanders accomplished two things in his *Paul and Palestinian Judaism*. First, in a thorough survey of Jewish literature, he provided a compelling argument that Palestinian Judaism is to be understood not as a religion of legalistic works-righteousness, but instead as one of 'covenantal nomism'. The law (*nomos* in Greek) functioned as the means by which faithful Jews maintained their membership in the covenant community of Israel, a covenant established through divine grace. Second, with respect to Paul, he argued that what Paul had to say about Judaism and the law should not be understood as an assessment that he had arrived at independently and apart from Christ. In particular, these statements should not be taken as a description of his experience of Judaism prior to his Damascus experience, and thus as a way of accounting for his shift from Torah to Christ. Rather, they should be seen as forms of argument that he developed in order to express and defend a more fundamental conviction – namely, that God had provided Jesus as a means of salvation for all, Jew and Gentile, on equal terms. To put it differently, Paul can be seen as a covenantal nomist who came to believe that Jesus was saviour and lord of all, and who drew the corollary that if salvation came through Christ, it could not come through Torah. Further, to understand the pattern of salvation that Christ has made available, Sanders argues that it is more fruitful to begin not with Paul's lawcourt metaphors (guilt–condemnation–justification) but with his participatory language – that is, the idea that the believer participates with Christ in a corporate process of dying to this age and rising to the life of the age to come.

To be sure, Sanders's work left a number of questions unanswered. Why, for example, did Paul draw a corollary (about the law) that other Jewish Christians (e.g. James and the Jerusalem church) did not? If one should reply that for Paul Gentiles are to be included on equal terms, one has just shifted the question to another point: What was the origin of Paul's belief in the universal scope of Christ's saving work? At the same time, however, Sanders's treatment of Paul's theme of 'justification by faith not works', especially his demonstration that this theme plays a very limited and specific role in Paul's letters, makes it difficult to answer this question simply by reverting to the older universalistic framework. Paul's conviction that Gentiles are to be included in the salvation made available in Christ is prior to, and the point of departure for, his language of 'justification by faith'. If Sanders is right, the linchpins of the older universalistic framework turn out to be secondary elements of some other framework, one in which 'Jew' and 'Gentile' and their relative status 'in Christ' represent more fundamental parts of the structure.

Of course, it would be a great oversimplification to say that Sanders has single-handedly demolished one interpretive framework and replaced it with another. For one thing, there have been various attempts to critique his approach and to argue for a new appreciation of old perspectives.[19] Further, to the extent that there has been a shift, resulting in the emergence of what James Dunn has called a 'new perspective on Paul',[20] others have had important parts to play.[21] In

[19] E.g. Stephen Westerholm, *Perspectives Old and New on Paul: The 'Lutheran' Paul and His Critics* (Grand Rapids: Eerdmans, 2004).

[20] James D. G. Dunn, 'The New Perspective on Paul', *Bulletin of the John Rylands Library* 65 (1983): 95–122.

[21] E.g. Johannes Munck, *Paul and the Salvation of Mankind* (London: SCM Press, 1959); Krister Stendahl, *Paul Among Jews and Gentiles* (Philadelphia: Fortress Press, 1976).

addition, among those who have been convinced by Sanders and have attempted to build on, amplify and refine his work, considerable variety of opinion can be discerned, especially pertaining to the matters of self-definition that are of interest to us here.

This is not the place to attempt anything like a description of the complicated post-Sanders map of Pauline interpretation. Instead, we will proceed by examining, in turn, the key components of self-definition in Paul (the Church, Torah religion, Israel), taking note of the various interpretive options as we go.

The Church and its constitution

Paul's statements about the Church can be interpreted in several possible ways. As has been indicated already, one of these is a thoroughgoing universalism – the idea that the Church is made up of generic human beings. Any distinction that might exist between Jew and Gentile is quite secondary and, in any case, has now become obsolete.

On the negative side of the ledger, no distinction is to be made between Jew and Gentile with respect to their plight under sin. 'All, both Jews and Greeks, are under the power of sin' (Rom. 3.9); God 'shows no partiality' towards sinners (Rom. 2.11–12); consequently, 'there is no distinction, since all have sinned' (Rom. 3.22–23). While Jews are differentiated by their possession of the law, the resultant difference is simply that the law serves to make the universal plight more apparent, in that 'through the law comes the knowledge of sin' (3.20; also 5.13; 7.7; Gal. 3.19), or even more severe, in that the law actually increased sin (Rom. 5.20; 7.5, 8, 11). Jewish claims that the law makes a positive difference are illusory (Rom. 2.17–24), and represent just one example of a universal human tendency to strive for righteousness on the basis of one's own merit and resources (Rom. 10.3).

On the positive side of the ledger, 'there is no distinction between Jew and Greek' in salvation either (Rom. 10.12). God is the God of both (3.29–30); Christ is both the 'Lord of all' (Rom. 10.12) and the one who 'has died for all' (2 Cor. 5.14–15), thereby making salvation available to 'everyone who calls on the name of the Lord' (Rom. 10.13). Paul's repeated use of 'everyone' or 'all' in such contexts (Rom. 5.18; 8.32; 10.4; 1 Cor. 15.22; Phil. 2.11) might well suggest that in his view the new community is generically universal. Even if a distinction might have existed in the past, now 'there is no longer Jew or Greek', because 'all of you are one in Christ Jesus' (Gal. 3.28).

Paul's argument in Galatians 3, however, leads us into another possible characterization of the Church. While verse 28 is much more well known than verse 29, it seems to be just a set-up for the conclusion to which the whole argument has been heading since 3.6–7. 'If you belong to Christ', Paul says to his Gentile readers, 'then you are Abraham's offspring' (literally 'seed'). The point of Paul's argument is not that the distinction between Jew and Gentile has become irrelevant in the light of some transcending universalism, but that Gentiles who believe in Christ thereby become full and equal members of Abraham's family. A similar conclusion, albeit arrived at by a different route, is found in Romans 4 (especially vv. 11–12, 16). We will have occasion to return to this point again, but for present purposes we need to note that this belongs to a collection of texts which might support the idea that for Paul the full identity of Israel has been taken over by the Church. If the community of Jews and Gentiles who believe in Christ thereby constitute the family of Abraham, then it may well be the case that for Paul, the Church is to be understood as the 'new Israel', a new community that has taken the place of old Israel in the purposes of God. In other words, Paul's view of the Church is thoroughly supersessionist.

Galatians itself contains two additional passages that might lend support to such a view. At the end of the letter Paul uses the term 'the Israel of God' with reference to those who are identified with the 'new creation' (6.16). If, as is quite plausibly the case, the reference is to the new community of Jewish and Gentile believers in Christ, then the verse provides us with explicit evidence of a 'new Israel' view of the Church. Earlier, in the allegory set out in 4.21—5.1, the focus shifts from Abraham to Sarah, as those who have been set free by Christ are characterized as children of Sarah. Further, in contrast to the children of Sarah, the free woman, those who are 'subject to the law' and are identified with 'the present Jerusalem' are children of Hagar, the slave. Since the children of Hagar are to be driven out and deprived of any share in the inheritance, the allegory might be read as a story of rejection and replacement: old Israel, Israel as defined by the law, has been driven out, while new Israel, brought into being by Christ, has received the full inheritance. Along the same lines, in Philippians Paul says to his Gentile readers that 'we . . . who boast in Christ Jesus' are 'the circumcision' (3.3), thereby ascribing to believers in Christ a term that he uses elsewhere with reference to the Jewish people themselves (Rom. 3.30; 4.12; 15.8; Gal. 2.7–9). In return, those who have been used to thinking of themselves as 'the circumcision' (*peritomē*) he describes instead as 'the mutilation' (*katatomē*; Phil. 3.2). In other words, in this line of interpretation Israel's real identity has now been taken over by the Church; old Israel, Israel according to the flesh, is left with just a debased parody of its identity.

If this were the whole story, we might have to conclude that for Paul the Church is a community in which the traditional distinctions between Jew and Gentile have been eradicated, the traditional markers of Jewish identity have been thoroughly reinterpreted, and any positive status that might have been enjoyed by the Israel of old has now passed – in this reinterpreted form and without remainder – to the Church. The Church is to be seen as 'new' or 'true' or 'spiritual' Israel. But this is not the whole story. Other statements in Paul's letters seem to suggest that 'Israel', 'Jew' and 'Gentile', in the traditional sense of these terms, continue to be significant categories for him, even within the Church.

One set of statements concerns Paul's own sense of his role as 'apostle to the Gentiles' (Rom. 11.13). While Paul has often been seen as the great champion of universalism, this self-description reflects a very Jewish way of viewing the world. Non-Jews did not think of themselves as 'Gentiles', any more than non-Greeks thought of themselves as barbarians (cf. Rom. 1.14). Paul did not describe himself as the apostle to 'everybody without distinction'. He describes himself as having been called by God to proclaim God's Son 'among the *Gentiles*' (Gal. 1.16), as having been sent 'to the *Gentiles*' (Gal. 2.9), as having 'received apostleship to bring about the obedience of faith among *all the Gentiles*' (Rom. 1.5), as having received grace 'to be a minister of Christ Jesus to the *Gentiles* in the priestly service of the gospel' (Rom. 15.16) – a self-description that implies the ongoing significance of 'Jew' and 'Gentile'.

In addition, Paul sees himself as a prime example of the Jewish remnant (Rom. 11.1–2), which leads to a second point. When he introduces the idea of a remnant a few chapters earlier (9.27–30), the emphasis falls on its smallness: 'though the number of the children of Israel were like the sand of the sea, only a remnant of them will be saved' (9.27, citing Isa. 10.22). In chapter 11, however, the emphasis is much more positive. The existence of the remnant demonstrates that God has not 'rejected his people' (11.1), which seems to suggest that for Paul the community of Jewish believers has intrinsic significance. In other words, even if Gentile believers enjoy equality of status with Jewish believers, these identities are not thereby abolished. The Church comprises two groups – a body of Jewish believers, who represent the remnant of Israel, and a body of Gentile believers, who have been called by God as well (9.24).

How did Gentiles get to be in this position? One possibility is that they have come in to replace those Israelites (the majority) who have been rejected. As we have seen, some material in Paul's letters might suggest a rejection–replacement model for the overall relationship between Israel and the Church. In addition, the olive tree analogy of Rom. 11.17–24 might suggest a variant of this for the Gentile portion of the Church more specifically. In this analogy Israel is represented as an olive tree and individual Israelites as its branches. The present situation is one in which 'some of the branches' have been 'broken off' and 'you [i.e. Gentile believers], a wild olive shoot' have been grafted in (11.17). The analogy seems to suggest a cause-and-effect situation. 'You will say', Paul says to his Gentile readers, '"Branches were broken off so that I might be grafted in"' (11.19 NRSV). He responds to this statement with a word (*kalōs*; lit. 'well') that might indicate assent. If the NRSV translation is accurate ('That is true'), Paul himself holds to a rejection–replacement understanding of his Gentile mission: all but the remnant of Israel are 'vessels of wrath made for destruction' (9.22), whose place on the olive tree has been taken by Gentiles who have been grafted 'in their place' (11.17 NRSV).

The NRSV translation, however, is not necessarily accurate here. For one thing, Paul says that the Gentile shoot has been grafted in *en autois*, which literally means 'among them'. Since he immediately goes on to say, 'and you have become a partner in the rich root of the olive tree', he seems to place emphasis on the relationship between the wild olive shoot and the branches that remain, rather than with the branches (only 'some') that have been broken off. Further, Paul's own response to the statement in verse 19 does not necessarily amount to an endorsement. He speaks only of faith, or its absence. His response could just as easily be read as a rejection of the notion: 'You will say, "Branches were broken off so that I might be grafted in." Well, they were broken off because of their unbelief, but you stand only through faith.' In other words, he might be rejecting the proposition that Gentile believers come in to take the place of Jews.

This suggests a different possibility for the status of the Gentiles – namely, that they have been added to the remnant of Jews who believe. The strongest piece of evidence for this idea is found in the rationale Paul gives later in Romans for the collection project. As he writes to the church in Rome, Paul is in the final stages of a project to collect money from his Gentile churches for the benefit of the church in Jerusalem (1 Cor. 16.1–4; 2 Cor. 7—9; Acts 19.21—21.19). In Romans 15.25–27 he describes this not only as an expression of generosity but also as an acknowledgement of indebtedness. Since Gentile believers have 'come to share in the spiritual blessings' belonging to the Jewish Church, they have become their 'debtors'. It is only right, then, that the Gentiles should 'be of service to them in material things'. Further evidence for this idea might be found in the statements that the gospel is 'to the Jew first, and also to the Greek' (Rom. 1.16) and that Christ became 'a servant of the circumcised . . . in order that the Gentiles might glorify God for his mercy' (Rom. 15.8–9 NRSV). Even in 1 Thessalonians 2.14–16, Paul's harsh denunciation of 'the Jews' serves the purpose of forging a close relationship ('imitators') between the Gentile Christians in Thessalonica and 'the churches of God in Christ Jesus that are in Judea'.

This suggests a scenario in which Gentiles come in to receive a share of the blessings that belong in the first instance to Israel, represented here by the remnant of Jewish believers. If so, then Paul may have understood his mission to the Gentiles within the framework of one of the 'patterns of universalism' already existing within the Jewish world, even if the framework was substantially reconfigured as a result of his new beliefs about Christ. There is considerable scholarly debate, however, as to whether he views his Gentile converts as Christian counterparts to the 'God-fearers,'[22] as beneficiaries of

[22] E.g. Mark D. Nanos, *The Mystery of Romans: The Jewish Context of Paul's Letter* (Minneapolis: Fortress Press, 1996).

the end-time redemption of Israel,[23] or as proselytes to a redefined family of Abraham.[24]

We will return to Paul's thinking about the Jewish remnant a little later, when we pick up the topic of the future salvation of Israel. Before we can do so, however, we need to consider Paul's treatment of contemporary Jewish religion.

Paul's critique of Torah religion and its contemporary adherents

Here we are not able to undertake even an introductory sketch of the complicated problem of 'Paul and the law'. Instead we will focus on his criticism of his Jewish contemporaries and the ways in which his use of the law in such contexts might be understood. We have already considered two aspects of Paul's criticism, one concerning the inability of the law to deal with sin and to provide salvation, and the other having to do with the law as a legalistic system of works-righteousness. Each of these, in different ways, raises the possibility that Paul simply misunderstood Torah religion. But other interpretations have been suggested.

One approach begins with Paul's belief that Jesus is Israel's Messiah (e.g. Rom. 9.5) and connects this with Jewish expectations concerning the nature and role of the Torah in the messianic age. Several scholars point to rabbinic traditions in which the Torah is seen as especially tailored to this age and the Messiah is expected to establish a new Torah in the age to come.[25] On this basis the suggestion has been made that Paul can simply be seen as a typical Jew who believes that the Messiah has come and thus that the age of the Torah is over. There was nothing wrong with it in its own time, but the Messiah has brought that time to an end. The essence of Paul's criticism then would be that his Jewish contemporaries have failed to recognize that the Messiah has come. The 'splendour' of the law has given

---

[23] E.g. E. P. Sanders, *Paul, the Law, and the Jewish People* (Philadelphia: Fortress Press, 1983), 171.

[24] As I argue in my *Paul and the Gentiles: Remapping the Apostle's Convictional World* (Minneapolis: Fortress Press, 1997).

[25] E.g. W. D. Davies, *Paul and Rabbinic Judaism* (London: SPCK, 1948), 71–2; Hans-Joachim Schoeps, *Paul: The Theology of the Apostle in the Light of Jewish Religious History* (Philadelphia: Westminster Press, 1961), 173.

way to the 'greater splendour' of Christ (2 Cor. 3.7–11); with the age of maturity, the period of the 'pedagogue' has come to an end (Gal. 3.24).

While this interpretation is attractive, it is nevertheless subject to criticism. Even if some changes might have been expected for the messianic age, it is difficult to imagine that a typical first-century Jew would have seen the function of the Torah in 'this age' simply as that of revealing sin, with no power to counteract it. To be sure, many of Paul's contemporaries lamented the presence of sin within Israel, and at least one near contemporary – the author of *4 Ezra* – even despaired of the possibility that people could keep the law in this age of sin. Still, *4 Ezra* was atypical; most Jews believed that the covenant provided an antidote to sin, that the law could be kept and that the solution to sin was repentance and a return to the law. The only possible parallel to Paul is provided by some Jewish writers who made similar statements not about Jews but about Gentiles: for those outside the covenant, the law functions simply to reveal sin and to demonstrate that God is just in his condemnation (e.g. *2 Baruch* 48.40–47; *Pseudo-Philo* 11.1–2). But in all of these writings the solution is for Gentiles to embrace the law and become part of the covenant people. In other words, even if there are some points of contact between Paul and his Jewish contemporaries with respect to the coming of the Messiah and the end of the age of sin, Paul is alone in aligning the law with the problem and not with the solution.

Another approach, identified with James Dunn, N. T. Wright and others, takes as its point of departure Sanders's observation that Paul uses the contrast between faith and works primarily to defend the inclusion of Gentiles in the community of believers. This approach goes beyond Sanders, however, by interpreting this as a fundamental criticism of contemporary Judaism rather than simply as a convenient debating tactic. 'Works of the law' are precisely those things (such as circumcision, food laws and so on) that differentiate Jews from Gentiles – what Dunn calls Jewish 'identity markers'.[26] In criticizing his Jewish contemporaries for putting their confidence in these things, Paul is objecting to the fact that they are using the Torah to reinforce

---

[26] James D. G. Dunn, *The New Perspective on Paul*, rev. edn (Grand Rapids: Eerdmans, 2005), 109.

a sense of their own ethnic superiority and to exclude the Gentiles from the sphere of God's saving purposes. Since God's promise to Abraham envisaged a single human family, a law that serves to create a line of demarcation within the human family cannot have any fundamental part to play in the consummation of God's promises and purpose. In a sense this interpretation overlaps with the previous one, in that it is the coming of Christ that brings to an end any Torah-based demarcation between one human group and another. But the emphasis on the role of the Torah in differentiating Jew from Gentile sets it apart.

Support for this reading of Paul can be found in what has been observed already, namely, that what Paul has in view when he speaks of the 'works of the law' are precisely those things that define the Jews as a distinct people. What differentiates this view from that of Sanders, however, is that it sees this aspect of Paul's discourse not simply as a handy, single-purpose argument to defend his Gentile mission but as a more fundamental criticism of Jewish self-understanding – or, at least, of an attitude characteristic of a highly nationalistic sub-group of Paul's Jewish contemporaries. What Paul is objecting to is not 'self-reliance' (as in the older framework) but 'national reliance' – 'a confidence that God is Israel's God, that possession of the law puts possessors in a position of advantage over all others, that the people marked out by circumcision are secure in God's praise'.[27]

Many Jewish readers of Paul, however, would find this interpretation no less problematical than its predecessors. For one thing, the 'confidence' described in the previous paragraph is precisely what covenantal nomism is all about – the belief that God has chosen Israel to be a special people, marked out from the other nations, a people called to maintain its distinct identity, to seek God's praise and to anticipate God's salvation. For Paul's contemporaries, such a self-understanding was not a fault but was precisely what characterized them as a covenant people. If this was what lay at the heart of Paul's Christ–Torah antithesis, then Paul was rejecting covenantal nomism itself and turning Jewish faithfulness into a fault.

[27] James D. G. Dunn, *The Theology of Paul the Apostle* (Edinburgh: T&T Clark, 1997; Grand Rapids: Eerdmans, 1998), 119.

But what about the idea that such a confidence in 'Israel's privileged status and restricted prerogative'[28] served to exclude the Gentiles? Certainly there were some Jews who took a very pessimistic attitude towards the Gentiles and the possibility of their salvation, but this was not the only – and probably not the dominant – view. We have already had occasion to observe that within the Judaism of Paul's day there were several 'patterns of universalism' – ways in which Jews were able to think of Gentiles as being included in God's purposes – each of which was fully consistent with their own covenantal self-understanding. If Paul's criticism of Torah religion is that it excludes Gentiles, then this represents just as much a misunderstanding of Judaism as does the idea that it is based on meritorious works-righteousness. If it be suggested that Paul's criticism was directed only at a particular ultra-nationalistic sub-group (or any other kind of sub-group), then it might be said in response that Paul has unfairly blamed the whole group for the excesses or faults of a few.

A third approach, initiated by Lloyd Gaston and developed further by a few others,[29] argues that for Paul the Torah continues to provide a valid means of righteousness for Jews, who are related to God through the covenant with Israel, while Christ represents another means of righteousness that God has provided for Gentiles, who necessarily stood outside the covenant relationship. Paul has no quarrel with the law itself, nor with Torah religion. Anything he has to say about the law has to do with the law as it pertains to Gentiles. His critical comments are directed against those who, by insisting that Gentiles need to adhere to the law, are failing to recognize that God has provided the Gentiles with a separate means of righteousness in Christ.

If this was indeed Paul's view, he would readily be absolved of any charge that his views were anti-Judaic or supersessionist. Still, it needs to be said that few interpreters have found Gaston's reading to be convincing. One difficulty emerges from something that has been

[28] Ibid., 355.

[29] Lloyd Gaston, 'Paul and the Torah', in *Antisemitism and the Foundations of Christianity*, ed. Alan T. Davies (New York and Toronto: Paulist Press, 1979), 48–71; John G. Gager, *The Origins of Anti-Semitism* (Oxford: Oxford University Press, 1983) and *Reinventing Paul* (Oxford: Oxford University Press, 2000); Stanley K. Stowers, *A Rereading of Romans: Justice, Jews, and Gentiles* (New Haven: Yale University Press, 1994).

observed already. Paul seems to ascribe positive value to the existence of a 'remnant' – Jews who believe in Jesus. If Gaston were correct, such a group would have represented a problem for Paul, not proof that God had not 'rejected his people' (Rom. 11.1).[30]

A final way in which the antithesis that Paul perceives between Christ and Torah might be accounted for within the so-called new perspective is to see it as rooted in the unexpected nature of Christ. For some, the key is the idea of a *crucified* Messiah. If, by raising Jesus from the dead, God has declared to be the Messiah someone upon whom the Torah pronounces a curse ('anyone hung on a tree is under God's curse'; Deut. 21.23), then Christ and Torah are in some way fundamentally at odds. For my part, I have argued that the answer is to be sought instead in the unexpected already–not-yet character of early beliefs about Jesus. In traditional messianic expectation, Torah and Messiah operated in different time periods: those who lived within the sphere of the Torah in this age would be vindicated by the Messiah when he came to establish the messianic age. In early Christian preaching, however, the Messiah has been identified in this age but his 'coming' to establish the messianic age is an event awaited in the future. How then is the community of the righteous to be identified in the period before the end – by adherence to the Torah or by faithfulness to Christ? When the two ages are sequential, there is no conflict between Torah and Messiah; but when they are perceived as overlapping, Christ and Torah might readily become rival ways of marking the boundary of the people destined for salvation.[31]

To the extent that they might prove to be valid, such approaches would help us understand how Paul arrived at the idea that Christ and Torah functioned in a rival way. But they do not provide much help with the question of Paul and anti-Judaism. For in his attempts to work out a scripturally based articulation of this Christ–Torah rivalry, Paul ends up describing Torah religion in ways that those who live within the sphere of the Torah would not recognize.

A more positive outcome, however, may be found in a third element of self-definition in Paul.

---

[30] See my 'Jewish Christianity, Israel's Stumbling and the *Sonderweg* Reading of Paul', *Journal for the Study of the New Testament* 29 (2006): 27–54.

[31] See further my *Paul and the Gentiles.*

'All Israel will be saved'

As we have observed from the outset, an important part of early Christian self-definition has to do with its views concerning scriptural Israel and the relationship that might exist between Israel and the Church. Much of what might be said in this regard with respect to Paul has been said already or, at the very least, might be inferred from it. One further aspect of Paul's thinking requires exploration, however – his declaration in Romans 11.26 that 'all Israel will be saved' and its role as the culmination of a discourse about Israel that began in Romans 9.1.

It is fair to say that a majority of interpreters understand 'Israel' here as a reference to ethnic Israel (the body of Jews as distinct from Gentiles) and 'salvation' as an event of the end-time. Before looking more closely at the ways in which Paul's declaration is understood within this group of interpreters, two other minority interpretations need to be noted.

In one of these, 'Israel' is understood as a reference to the Church, the new family of Abraham comprising Jewish and Gentile believers in Christ. This was Calvin's interpretation, and among its more modern advocates is N. T. Wright. Certainly, as we have seen, Paul can make statements consistent with the idea that for him the Church is a kind of 'new Israel' – statements in which 'he has systematically transferred the privileges and attributes of "Israel" to the Messiah and his people'.[32] Still, throughout Romans 11 'Israel' is defined not only in ethnic terms – Paul himself is 'an Israelite' (11.1); 'Israel' stands in contrast to 'the Gentiles', including Gentile believers (11.11) – but also in unrestricted terms – 'Israel' includes both 'the elect' and 'the rest' (11.7). Most interpreters disagree with Wright's interpretation and feel that if Paul's way of responding to the charge that 'God has rejected his people' Israel (11.1) is to redefine 'Israel' in this way, his response rings hollow and his 'great sorrow' for his 'kindred according to the flesh' (9.2–3) turns out to be a case of crocodile tears.

In the other minority interpretation, 'Israel' is understood in ethnic terms, but 'all Israel' is seen as the cumulative total of Jews

---

[32] N. T. Wright, *The Climax of the Covenant: Christ and the Law in Pauline Theology* (Edinburgh: T&T Clark; Minneapolis: Fortress Press, 1991), 250.

who come to believe in Christ up to the time of Christ's coming, rather than as a larger group that will be 'saved' when 'the Deliverer' comes at the end.[33] Perhaps the strongest argument in favour of this reading is that while verse 26 is often read as if Paul were saying 'and *then* all Israel will be saved' – i.e. at the time of the end – what he actually says is 'and *so* all Israel will be saved' – a term having to do with manner rather than with timing. Still, a temporal sequence seems to be in view in verse 25: the 'hardening' that characterizes the unbelieving part of Israel is a situation that will last '*until* the full number of the Gentiles has come in'. Most interpreters understand this as a statement that when the Gentile mission has reached its completion, then the Messiah will come, the 'hardening' will be removed and 'all Israel will be saved'.

Nevertheless, significant differences are present within this larger group of interpreters as well. One question has to do with the force of 'all'. Most interpreters understand it as a reference to Israel as a total corporate entity rather than to a group comprising every individual Jewish person, though the word could be taken in the latter sense. More significant differences arise, however, with respect to the relationship between 'all Israel' and Christ. At one end of the interpretive spectrum, this end-time salvation of Israel is understood as it would have been in traditional Jewish expectation – as an act of God's faithfulness to the covenant made with Israel. In other words, Israel's salvation is not accomplished by Christ or linked to Christ in any essential way (except perhaps as Israel's expected Messiah). This reading is most characteristic of Gaston's dual-covenant approach, but it is not restricted to it. The most compelling argument in favour of such a reading is the complete absence of any explicit reference to Christ in the whole of Romans 11. Still, the chapter is the culmination of a larger argument, one in which the question of how Israel might be 'saved' is carried out with explicit reference to Christ (10.1–13).

Interpreters at the other end of the spectrum understand Paul's statement as envisaging a mass conversion of individual Jews

33 So Christopher Zoccali, '"And So All Israel Will be Saved": Competing Interpretations of Romans 11.26 in Pauline Scholarship', *Journal for the Study of the New Testament* 30 (2008): 289–318. Zoccali provides a helpful survey of the various interpretations of Romans 1.25–26.

to Christ in the end-times. At this point, then, 'all Israel' is simply incorporated into the Church, the new people of God in which there is no longer any distinction between Jew and Gentile, and thus does not continue to have any separate identity or significance.

Lying in between are approaches in which the ultimate salvation of 'all Israel' is seen to be centred in Christ, but Israel nevertheless continues to exist as a distinct and significant entity. The present 'remnant' is simply the 'first fruits' of the whole (11.16). In the present, the Jewish remnant continues to have a distinct identity, so that the people of God consists of two groups – Jewish believers, who belong by nature to the 'olive tree' of Israel, and Gentiles, who have come in to share the 'spiritual blessings' (15.27) that properly belong to the Jewish people. In this reading, the people of God has the same two-fold structure in the end-times, except that the remnant has now been expanded to include 'all Israel'.

These differences notwithstanding, however, the most significant observation is this: except for the minority positions described above, the implication of the remaining interpretations is that Israel – the community of those identified by their adherence to the Torah and not by belief in Christ – continues to have some sort of validity. If 'the gifts and calling of God are irrevocable' (11.29), so that 'all Israel will be saved' in the end, then Israel as a distinct entity continues to have theological significance in the present.

The question of Christian self-definition for Paul, then, is complex. Statements that he makes in his letters about the pertinent dimensions of the question – the constitution of the Church, the shortcomings of Torah-religion, the future of Israel – are open to a variety of interpretations. Further, it seems to be very difficult to arrive at a consistent position that takes account of everything Paul has to say without resorting to special pleading or forced interpretations. Loose ends and tensions seem to be present in every interpretive position. For some interpreters, however, this is an important point. While it might seem that Paul's new Christian convictions would have led logically to conclusions that negated Jewish identity and Israel's significance, Paul's commitment to his native convictions remained sufficiently strong that he was unwilling to sacrifice them to logic and was fully prepared to live with the resulting tensions.

Social location of Paul and his intended readers

If we were to consider each of Paul's letters, our discussion in this section (social location) and the next (rhetorical function) would be lengthy and complicated indeed. In this chapter, however, we are interested in Paul himself and his letters as a whole, and thus can afford to be briefer.

In some ways the issue of social location is much clearer with respect to Paul and his readers than it was with the Gospels and Acts. Here we know the identity of the author, or at least the most important of the letters that bear Paul's name. In addition, even though the letters contain lengthy sections of theological discourse, they are also very personal letters, revealing a considerable amount of biographical information and insight. Further, in the Acts of the Apostles we have a connected narrative of Paul's life and activity, from his initial persecution of the Christian movement and his call to be an apostle, through his mission activity from Damascus to Greece, and on to his imprisonment in Rome. Whereas with the Gospels and Acts we had, at best, only indirect and inferential information about the identity and ethnicity of the author and the intended recipients, and about the date of the writing, here we are on much firmer ground.

Still, there are elements of complexity and uncertainty. One has to do with the account in Acts. Differences in detail (e.g. the visit to Jerusalem in Acts 9.26–30 and Gal. 1.18–24) and in overall presentation (e.g. Paul's initiative in having Timothy circumcised (Acts 16.3; cf. Gal. 2.1–10); the differing attitude towards law observance in Acts 21.24 and Gal. 2.11–14) raise questions about the reliability of Acts as a historical account, whether the author was acquainted with Paul (despite the first-person narrative in 16.11–17; 20.5—21.17; and 27.1—28.16) and whether he even knew Paul's letters, which are not mentioned at all.[34]

Further questions emerge with respect to Paul himself, especially with respect to the nature of what has traditionally been called his 'conversion'. In both scholarly discourse and popular imagination,

[34] On this and other related issues, see a more complete account in my 'Introduction to the Pauline Corpus', in *The Oxford Bible Commentary*, ed. John Barton and John Muddiman (Oxford: Oxford University Press, 2001), 1062–83.

Paul's experience has commonly been understood as a conversion, even as the prototypical example of conversion – a transformation in which he left one religion (Judaism) and joined another (Christianity). More recently this conception has been challenged in two ways. One is the recognition that the separation of the Christian movement from its Jewish matrix was a long process, so that in Paul's day it is not appropriate to think in terms of two separate religions. The other is the observation that when Paul speaks of this experience (e.g. Gal. 1.13–16; 1 Cor. 15.8–11), he presents it as an event in which he was called to be an apostle, describing it in terms associated not with conversion but with the call of a prophet (e.g. Isa. 49.1; Jer. 1.5). This raises the possibility that Paul's transformation should be understood as a call or a commissioning, rather than a conversion – that is, that on both sides of the event Paul was a Jew who served the same God, but that he had been called by God to a new task (to 'proclaim [God's Son] among the Gentiles'; Gal. 1.16).[35] At the same time, however, there are many who feel that Paul's experience constituted a much more dramatic shift in basic convictions and social allegiances than was ever the case with an Amos or a Jeremiah. If so, with the proper definition and qualifications, conversion might continue to be an appropriate category.[36]

Another way of posing the question about the nature of Paul's transformation is to focus on his Gentile mission and the nature of 'the gospel that I proclaim among the Gentiles' (Gal. 2.2). Did his interest in the Gentiles result from a new conviction that any distinction between Jew and Gentile had been abolished in Christ, or was it a revised version of one of the 'patterns of universalism' that were already current in his Jewish world? In other words, are we to understand his transformation as an abandonment of Judaism and Jewish particularism, or as a reinterpretation of Judaism and Jewish universalism?

However we are to understand Paul's transformative experience, further questions can be raised about his starting point. What kind of Jew was he? From his letters it is readily apparent that he was a diaspora Jew. At the same time, however, he presents himself as

[35] See Stendahl, *Paul Among Jews and Gentiles*, 7–23.

[36] E.g. Alan F. Segal, *Paul the Convert: The Apostolate and Apostasy of Saul the Pharisee* (New Haven: Yale University Press, 1990).

a Pharisee (Phil. 3.5), one who was 'more exceedingly a zealot for the traditions of my ancestors' than many of his contemporaries (Gal. 1.14). Depending on how they choose to weigh the evidence, interpreters have variously placed Paul at a variety of points along the Jewish spectrum – from the conservative Pharisaic school of Shammai at one end, to a radically Hellenized Jew on the far side of Philo at the other.

A related question has to do with his degree of contentment with his Jewish way of life prior to his Damascus experience. In the past it has been common to read Romans 7, with its account of the desperate situation of those who live 'under the law' ('wretched man that I am!'; 7.24) as a description of Paul's own previous experience. If this is a legitimate reading, then even before his 'conversion', Paul had already come to the conviction that Torah religion was inadequate, unworkable or otherwise problematical (because it was based on works? because the law was powerless to deal with sin? because it excluded the Gentiles?). For many reasons, most of them surveyed in the previous section, others feel that such a reading is not legitimate, that the 'I' of Romans 7 is not Paul himself, but a rhetorical device to speak of something else (the experience of Adam; the human experience viewed from the perspective of someone 'in Christ'; the Gentiles; and so on). A more accurate picture might be found in Paul's retrospective statement in Philippians 3.6: 'as to righteousness under the law, [I was] blameless'. If we start with this latter picture, Paul's transformation would consist instead in a new estimation about Christ, so that any negative comments about Judaism or Torah religion would be corollaries of his new beliefs, rather than contributing causes.

Further questions emerge with respect to Paul's relationship with the world of Judaism after his transformative experience. On the one hand, many pieces of evidence might suggest that he lived and carried out his apostolic mission entirely in the non-Jewish world. He describes himself as the 'apostle to the Gentiles' (e.g. Rom. 11.13); his task was to 'go to the Gentiles', while Peter and others went 'to the circumcised' (Gal. 2.7–9; also 1 Thess. 2.16; Rom. 1.5; 15.15–19); he takes it as a matter of principle that he and other Jewish believers should be prepared to 'live like a Gentile', at least when associating with Gentile believers (Gal. 2.14); his letters, for the most part, are addressed to a non-Jewish readership (e.g. 1 Cor. 12.2; Gal. 4.8;

1 Thess. 1.9). At the same time, however, he reveals that on five occasions he 'received from the Jews the forty lashes minus one' (2 Cor. 11.24) – a form of synagogue discipline to which he would have been subject only if he had chosen to identify himself in some way with local Jewish communities. Despite his identity as the apostle to the Gentiles, he also declares his willingness to live like a Jew 'in order to win Jews' (1 Cor. 9.20) and hopes that his own ministry to the Gentiles will provoke jealousy among his own people 'and thus save some of them' (Rom. 11.13–14). Again we are faced with the question of how to balance conflicting evidence pertaining to an issue that affects how we understand Paul's negative statements about Judaism and Torah religion.

This leads into related questions about the social location of Paul's communities. Again there is a tension between the picture that emerges from Acts and material in Paul's own letters. In Acts, Paul typically begins his mission in each new city by preaching in the synagogue. This produces mixed results: while some Jews, together with a larger number of Gentile synagogue adherents ('God-fearers'), respond positively to the message, many Jews are vigorously opposed to it. Jewish opposition eventually forces Paul to withdraw from the synagogue and to establish a separate Christian group containing a mixture of Jews, God-fearers and new Gentile converts. In Paul's own letters, however, we find no explicit indication that the communities addressed contained any Jewish members at all (except for Romans 16, addressed to a congregation that he did not found). As we have seen, Paul frequently addresses his readers collectively in terms that seem to apply exclusively to non-Jews.

Still, the evidence from the letters is not unambiguous. As we have seen, Paul also seems to be interested in 'winning' Jews. Also, the frequency with which he cites Scripture in his letters indicates that he can assume considerable familiarity with Jewish Scripture on the part of his converts, which is at least consistent with the idea that many of them had been attracted to the synagogue before they had responded to his gospel. Further, if the persecution experienced by the Thessalonians (1 Thess. 2.14–16) was at the hands of the local Jewish community – as might be indicated by the otherwise unprompted comparison to the situation of believers in Judea – then this community at least existed in some sort of relationship with the synagogue. Finally, Paul spent a considerable portion of his time and energy organizing a financial collection among his churches for the benefit of the 'saints at Jerusalem' (Rom. 15.25–31; 1 Cor. 16.1–4; 2 Cor. 8—9; cf. Gal. 2.10), which indicates that a relationship existed (or at least that Paul felt it should exist) between his churches and the community of Jewish believers in Jerusalem.

It is readily apparent, then, that interpreters are faced with a whole bundle of decisions pertaining to the location of Paul and his communities with respect to the synagogue and the Jewish world. How we assess the nature of Paul's 'anti-Judaic' statements and discourses will depend to a significant extent on how we resolve these interpretive decisions. While our purpose here is more to identify and analyse them than to resolve them, it should be clear that questions concerning social location are closely intertwined with questions concerning self-definition, as discussed at greater length in the preceding section.

But what about the function of these 'anti-Judaic' statements and discourses in the letters themselves?

Rhetorical function of Paul's treatment of Jews and Judaism

Lloyd Gaston is right at least to this extent: everything Paul has to say about Jews and Judaism is in letters addressed to Gentile churches. Even if it should be the case that there was a Jewish element, Paul chooses to conceive of his churches as Gentile. His comments about Jews and Judaism are third-party references in letters addressed to non-Jewish believers in Christ, even if on occasion he addresses a fictional Jewish debating partner (e.g. Rom. 2.17–29) to further his argument. However we understand his comments about Jews and Judaism, they appear in letters whose primary purpose is to build up Gentile churches – to reinforce their basic identity and self-understanding; to provide teaching and guidance; to address problems and dangers; and so on. The question here, then, has to do with the way in which his comments about Jews and Judaism function with respect to this purpose – and what we are to make of it.

Speaking in general terms, we can identify at least four rhetorical contexts in which such comments appear: encouragement of Gentile believers who are experiencing persecution at the hands of their (possibly Jewish) fellow-citizens (1 Thess. 2.14–16); warning against attempts by outsiders to persuade Gentile believers to adopt circumcision and other aspects of Torah observance (Galatians; Philippians 3); reflection on the nature of apostolic life and the 'greater glory' attending the 'ministers of a new covenant' (2 Corinthians 3); and apologetic self-introduction, as Paul prepares for a visit to a church he did not found by defending his gospel against Jewish (and Jewish-Christian) criticisms on the one hand and Gentile attitudes of superiority and over-confidence on the other (Romans).

If Gaston is also right in his larger argument – that Paul has little to say about Jews and Judaism per se, but that his comments about the law have to do only with the way in which the law impinges on those who are outside the covenant with Israel – then no charge of anti-Judaism or supersessionism can legitimately be applied to him. Few interpreters, however, are willing to follow Gaston down this road. In our assessment of these passages, then, we probably need to reckon with the fact that in order to achieve his purposes with respect to his Gentile congregations, Paul makes comments that pertain directly to Torah religion and its adherents.

Of course, any assessment of this material would depend to a significant extent on decisions made by interpreters in response to questions explored in the previous two sections. The question of rhetorical function, however, adds another question to the interpretive mix. What balance should we strike between Paul's own intentions on the one hand and the actual effects of his rhetoric with respect to his Gentile readers on the other?

Concluding observations

As was the case with the Gospels and Acts, our assessment of Paul's letters with respect to issues of antisemitism, anti-Judaism and supersessionism will depend on where we locate him with respect to our three axes (self-definition, social location, rhetorical function). In some ways, the situation is simpler in this case. Here we have much more explicit information about the identity and life-situation of the author and his intended readers than was the case in previous chapters. Nevertheless, the fact that we are dealing with letters whose author is Jewish and whose intended readers are Gentile means that in other ways the situation is trickier. In addition to the kind of interpretive questions encountered in previous chapters, here we also have to reckon with questions involving a balance of perspectives: the situation looks different from the perspective of the Jewish author than it does from that of his Gentile readers. Put differently, the balance that needs to be struck has to do with the intentions of the author and the effects of his writings.

On the one side of things, interpreters can begin with Paul himself and emphasize the Jewish side of the balance. Paul is thoroughly Jewish and thus can hardly be accused of antisemitism or even anti-Judaism. His expressed hope for the future salvation of 'all Israel' may well represent the most positive and non-supersessionist statement in the whole New Testament. He can portray his apostolic task as having to do with bringing non-Jews into the family of Abraham, making it possible for them to share the rich blessings that belong in the first instance to Jews. He can portray his message as having to do with the fulfilment of promises that God made at the outset to Abraham and reiterated 'through his prophets in the holy scriptures' (Rom. 1.2).

On the other side of things, interpreters can begin with Paul's readers and emphasize the Gentile side of the balance. In his letters, Gentile readers encountered a portrait of Torah religion that no Jew would recognize and that would inevitably produce misapprehension and misunderstanding. Further, Paul's argument that simply by being 'in Christ' Gentiles were members of Abraham's 'seed' could readily be understood in a supersessionist way, especially in a Gentile context where there were few Jewish 'branches' with whom they were called on to share – and even more especially as time went on and the Christian movement became increasingly Gentile. In addition, Paul himself was a major contributor to this demographic shift. Not only was he the most successful early missionary to the Gentiles, but his teaching about Torah religion gave him a reputation among Jews (e.g. Acts 21.21) that, through a form of 'guilt by association', made it increasingly difficult for Jewish Christians who were more Torah-observant to remain within the Jewish world.

This leads us into the matter of the 'afterlife' of the early Christian writings and their incorporation into a new entity – the New Testament – to which we will return in the final chapter.

6

The New Testament Then and now

The remaining writings of the New Testament

In the previous chapters we considered the documents that have figured most prominently in the scholarly discussion of antisemitism, anti-Judaism, supersessionism and the New Testament – namely, Matthew, Luke–Acts, John and the undisputed epistles of Paul. This, of course, does not exhaust the topic. Other New Testament writings – especially Mark, the other epistles that bear Paul's name, Hebrews, 1 Peter and Revelation – contain material germane to the topic. Including these would certainly have made for a more complete account, enriching our discussion with further detail and additional genres of literature (e.g. Revelation as an apocalypse, Hebrews as a sermon or homiletic exhortation). Still, as is evident from the works of Isaac, Baum and Ruether, the writings that we have considered are the most significant for our topic; in addition, they represent the core of the New Testament. Given the introductory nature of this book, then, it seemed advisable to concentrate on the most significant writings and to provide a relatively thorough survey of the divergencies in scholarly interpretation and the exegetical decision points on which they are based. Here we will content ourselves with a few brief comments on some of the other writings.

The Gospel of Mark contains material that certainly could be read in an anti-Jewish manner. Isaac notes the way in which Mark's account of Jesus' trial and crucifixion ascribes greater culpability to the Jewish leaders than to Pilate.[1] For example, Mark depicts Pilate's offer to release Jesus as stemming from his perception that the Jewish leaders were motivated more by their envy of Jesus than by any specific legal infraction (15.1–15). In his response, Baum touches on a number of

[1] Jules Isaac, *Jesus and Israel* (New York: Holt, Rinehart & Winston, 1971), 295, 324.

additional aspects that, in his view, might be adduced as evidence of an anti-Jewish outlook:[2] Jesus' statement that he taught in parables so that, except for the disciples, his hearers would not understand and thus would not be forgiven (4.10–12); the cursing of the fig tree (11.12–14, 20–21), which brackets the account of Jesus' demonstration in the Temple (11.15–19) and which thus could be interpreted as a message of rejection and destruction; the parable of the tenants (12.1–12), in which the unworthy tenants are destroyed and the vineyard given to others; the tearing of the veil of the Temple (15.38); the acclamation of Jesus as 'Son of God' by the Gentile centurion (15.39); and so on. Nevertheless, whatever latent anti-Judaism might be present in this material, Mark displays little inclination to draw it out and make it explicit. More generally, Mark's Gospel does not contain the kind of sustained reflection on Jesus' significance for Israel, the Gentiles and the Church that we have seen in the other Gospels. Most scholars believe that Mark served as one of the sources for Matthew and Luke, which means that the significance of this Gospel for our topic has to do more with the way in which he provided material that could be the object of such reflection than with the Gospel itself.

In addition to the epistles that served as the focus of discussion in Chapter 5, there are six other epistles that, while bearing Paul's name, also display features of vocabulary, style and patterns of thought that are uncharacteristic of Paul, which has led a majority of scholars to doubt that they were written by Paul directly. To be sure, the degree of doubt is not uniform. At one end of the spectrum stand 2 Thessalonians and Colossians, which a number of scholars are prepared to attribute to Paul. At the other are 1 Timothy and Titus, with Ephesians and 2 Timothy standing close by. Further information on these epistles, their characteristics and origins can be found in any standard New Testament introduction or Bible dictionary.

These epistles contain a few passages that might be considered anti-Judaic. The most blatant is the statement in Titus that 'there are also many rebellious people, idle talkers and deceivers, especially those of the circumcision', people who propagate 'Jewish myths' and 'must

[2] Gregory Baum, *The Jews and the Gospel: A Re-Examination of the New Testament* (Westminster, Md.: Newman Press, 1961), 30–7.

be silenced' (Titus 1.10–11, 14 NRSV). It might be noted in passing that the author is perhaps even more disparaging of the residents of Crete than he is of the Jews (1.12–13). In Colossians, regulations 'of food and drink' and the observance 'of festivals, new moons, or sabbaths' are treated as 'only a shadow of what is to come', whose 'substance belongs to Christ' (2.16–17). The fact that these observances are not completely devalued but are given the status at least of a 'shadow', together with other considerations from the context (see the next point), make it probable that Jewish practices are in view. Still, whatever value these practices might have had, clearly they represent the inferior part of a shadow/reality dualism and have now been superseded by Christ. The statement a few verses earlier that those who 'were buried with him [Christ] in baptism' have thereby been 'circumcised with a circumcision not made with hands' (2.11–12) seems to partake in the same pattern of literal/spiritual dualism. In Ephesians, the Jewish law, 'with its commandments and ordinances', is presented as a 'dividing wall', which in the past served to separate Jew from Gentile and thus to create 'hostility' but which has now been 'abolished' in Christ, with the result that the two groups have become 'one new humanity in place of the two' (2.14–16). Further, this 'new humanity' seems to have taken over the identity of scriptural Israel. The Gentiles, who used to be 'aliens from the commonwealth of Israel and strangers to the covenants of promise', now 'have been brought near by the blood of Christ' (2.11–13) – which seems to imply that the new community of Jews and Gentiles now represents the 'commonwealth of Israel'. In most of these epistles Paul's role as apostle to the Gentiles receives particular attention (Col. 1.25–29; Eph. 3.6–8; 1 Tim. 2.7; 2 Tim. 4.17).

In Colossians, the depiction of the religion of Israel as a shadow that has now given way to the reality brought by Christ is just a passing image, one theological construct among many. In the epistle to the Hebrews, by contrast, it is the dominant motif. Hebrews presents itself as a 'word of exhortation' (13.22), written to a group of readers who are facing persecution and suffering at the hands of non-Christians (12.3–4; 13.13) and who, the author fears, are in danger of 'drift[ing] away from' (2.1) the faith they had once held with 'confidence' (10.35). To bolster their faith and shore up their confidence, the author carries out a systematic comparison between Jesus, together with the 'new and living way that he has opened for us' (10.20), and the institutions and officers of the 'first covenant' which is now 'obsolete and . . . will soon disappear' (8.13—9.1). Jesus, the 'mediator of a new covenant' (9.15), is superior to the angels who mediated the first one (2.1–2), to Moses (3.1–6), to Joshua (4.8) and to the high priest (5.1–10). The 'new covenant' (8.13) provides a better sabbath rest (4.8–10), a better sanctuary (9.6–12) and a more effective sacrifice for sin (9.25–26). For the author of Hebrews, the old is not devoid of value. But it is just a shadow of the reality that has been fully realized in the new: 'the law has only a shadow of the good things to come and not the true form of these realities' (10.1 NRSV). Now that the 'true form' has arrived, the old has become 'obsolete' (8.13): Christ 'abolishes the first in order to establish the second' (10.9). In short, the institutions of scriptural Israel have been superseded by Christ.

The issue presented by the epistle to the Hebrews, then, is this message of supersessionism. The writing contains no direct polemic against the Jewish people of the author's own day. Indeed, the supersessionist argument centres on Jewish institutions rather than on the Jewish people; there is no explicit statement to the effect that the Church has taken over the identity and heritage of Israel.[3] Still, it would be just a short step from the one to the other; a supersession of institutions may well be taken to imply a supersession of peoples. If the Temple is but a shadow of the reality that has appeared with Christ, a reader of the epistle could readily conclude that a similar relationship must exist between the people of the Temple and the people of Christ. What this would mean for a reader of the epistle is complicated by a lack of clarity concerning the ethnic identity of the intended readers. As its title indicates, the epistle has traditionally been understood as having been addressed to Jewish Christians who, facing renewed persecution for their faith, are tempted to return to the synagogue. This traditional reading finds some support in the statement that 'the children whom God has given me [Jesus]' are 'the descendants of Abraham' (2.13, 16). If this interpretation is correct, then the supersessionism of Hebrews represents a dispute between Jews about the true meaning and purpose of Israel's institutions.

[3] See Lloyd Kim, *Polemic in the Book of Hebrews: Anti-Semitism, Anti-Judaism, Supersessionism?* Princeton Theological Monograph Series (Eugene, Or.: Pickwick, 2006).

There is no clear indication in the epistle, however, that the readers are tempted to return to the synagogue. The danger is simply that they might 'grow weary or lose heart' (12.3) and '[turn] away from the living God' (3.12; also 2.1; 3.13; 6.4–6) – something that could just as easily apply to Gentiles. To the extent that the intended readership of the epistle included or consisted of Gentiles, its supersessionism could easily slide over into anti-Judaism.

The First Letter of Peter is also written to communities facing persecution 'for the name of Christ' (4.14), but here there is no doubt about the ethnic identity of the intended readers. Before coming to Christ they spent their time 'in doing what the Gentiles like to do' (4.3); now they have been 'ransomed from the futile ways inherited from [their] ancestors' (1.18 NRSV). Neither description would have been appropriate for Jews. Clearly they are Gentiles – or, at least, this is what they used to be. Now that they have taken on the name of Christ, the author considers them to be Gentiles no longer: 'conduct yourselves honourably among the Gentiles' (2.12). What, then, have they become? While the author in one instance refers to his readers as 'Christian' (4.16), he most characteristically describes them in terms borrowed from scriptural depictions of Israel. The letter as a whole is addressed 'to the exiles of the dispersion' (1.1), language that echoes Israel's diaspora experience (also 1.17; 2.11). 'You are a chosen race, a royal priesthood, a holy nation, a people for God's possession', he says in 2.9, ascribing to them terms used of Israel in Exodus 19.6 and Isaiah 43.20–21. Christian wives have become 'daughters [of Sarah]' (3.6).

What is striking about this language is the casual, unreflective way in which it is used. The author seems simply to take for granted that terms describing the identity of Israel can, without further ado, be transferred to the Gentile Church.

While the book of Revelation is also addressed to believers suffering persecution, unlike Hebrews and 1 Peter it is marked by sharp polemic against those whom the author holds responsible for the persecution. The primary target of the polemic is Babylon (14.8; 16.19; 17.5; 18.2, 10, 21), in all probability a code name for Rome. The harshness of the language is troubling for many readers: 'they will also drink the wine of God's wrath, poured unmixed into the cup of his anger, and they will be tormented with fires and sulphur in the presence of the holy angels and in the presence of the Lamb.

And the smoke of their torment goes up for ever and ever' (Rev. 14.10–11 NRSV). But even if Rome is primarily in view, polemical language is directed against Jews as well. The letter to the church in Smyrna speaks of 'the slander on the part of those who say that they are Jews and are not, but are a synagogue of Satan' (2.9 NRSV). A similar phrase appears in the letter to the church in Philadelphia: 'those of the synagogue of Satan who say that they are Jews and are not, but are lying' (3.9 NRSV). Later in the book the author describes Jerusalem as 'the great city that is prophetically called Sodom and Egypt, where also their Lord was crucified' (11.8 NRSV). While some allowances might be made for literature written by those who are suffering persecution – references to persecution are found in each passage (2.9–10; 3.8–10; 11.7–10) – the harshness of the language raises questions that are pertinent to this study.[4]

Any full investigation of these questions – and those raised by anti-Judaic material in the other literature just surveyed – would involve the same considerations that have guided our investigation in previous chapters: the patterns of self-definition present in each work; the social location of the author and intended readers; the rhetorical function of the pertinent material within the work as a whole. While these writings are certainly not to be disregarded, it is also the case that a full study would not add anything qualitatively different from the results that have emerged from the previous chapters.

But there is a further aspect of the New Testament that requires consideration.

The emergence of the New Testament as a canonical whole

To this point we have been considering individual writings contained in the New Testament. But the ongoing significance of these writings stems from the fact that they have been preserved as part of a larger collection. None of the original authors wrote with this intention or with the awareness of such a possibility. The fact that these

---

[4] See Philip L. Mayo, *'Those Who Call Themselves Jews': The Church and Judaism in the Apocalypse of John*, Princeton Theological Monograph Series (Eugene, Or.: Pickwick, 2006).

originally stand-alone writings are of interest and significance today stems from a subsequent development – a process of collection and selection that resulted in the emergence of the 'New Testament' as the second component of a two-part canon of Christian Scripture. This development has added another layer or dimension that needs to be considered in its own right.

This is not the place to discuss the development of the canon in any detail; concise accounts can be found in standard Bible dictionaries and New Testament introductions. For our purposes, however, it is important to observe several aspects of the context in which this development took place. For convenience, we can use the same three axes that proved to be useful in the preceding chapters.

Social location

While distinctively Jewish-Christian groups continued to exist well into the third century and beyond, the New Testament canon emerged in a Church that was self-consciously Gentile in its composition and outlook. A typical example is provided by Tertullian, who was also one of the key figures in the development of the canon; among his contributions to the development was the term 'new testament' itself (e.g. *Against Marcion* 4.1). Writing early in the third century, he declares: '[God] promised that out of the womb of Rebecca "two peoples and two nations were about to proceed" [Gen. 25.23] – of course, those of the Jews, that is, of Israel; and of the Gentiles, that is, ours' (*Answer to the Jews* 1.3). Tertullian simply assumes – and the assumption was widespread – that the Christian Church is a Gentile institution, existing outside of and fully separated from the world of Judaism. This means that the New Testament as a whole emerged in quite a different social location from that of its parts. In the first century, 'Christianity' and 'Judaism' did not exist as clearly distinct entities; with respect to individual Christian writings, there often is uncertainty about the ethnic makeup of the communities addressed and the degree to which they had become separated from the Jewish world. By the end of the second century, however, there seems to be no uncertainty, at least from the perspective of those who were in the process of recognizing such writings as authoritative Scripture. Clear boundaries were drawn between Christianity and Judaism; the process of separation had fully run its course and the Church was now definitively Gentile.

To be sure, as is demonstrated by Tertullian himself (and in more than one way), the canon emerged in a situation of diversity and conflict, where various Christian groups engaged in competition for members and influence. Tertullian wrote a major treatise against one of these groups (the Marcionites) and later joined another (the Montanists). In addition, there were – as we have observed – various forms of Jewish Christians, along with a variety of Gnostic groups. The New Testament canon emerged within one of these groups, a group that considered itself to be 'orthodox' or 'catholic' (in contrast to other groups that it labelled 'heretical') and that worked energetically to establish its claim to be the sole legitimate heir of the apostolic tradition. Indeed, one of the instruments used in the service of this claim was the idea of 'New Testament' itself. Along with two other developments – a church structure built around localized bishops, considered to be the legitimate successors of the apostles; and a 'rule of faith', short, creed-like summaries of Christian belief – the idea of a canon of Scripture in two 'testaments' functioned as one of three pillars of an emerging authority structure.

Self-definition

The New Testament as an authoritative collection, then, emerged as part of a process of self-definition within one segment of Gentile Christianity. In this process of self-definition, the relationship between catholic Christianity and the Israel of the 'Old Testament' emerged as an important issue. On one side, catholic Christianity differentiated itself from Jewish Christians who continued to observe the law and ascribed theological value to their ethnic identity. On the other were Marcion and the Gnostics. Marcion, of course, rejected Israel's Scriptures entirely. In his view, the God of Israel – the god who created the material world and gave the law – is an inferior deity, a god of harsh judgement who is fully distinct from the Father God proclaimed by Christ. Consequently, he rejected any idea of a connection or continuity between Israel and those who believed in Christ. In his view, these two groups were as distinct and separate as the gods whom they worshipped. The thought of the Gnostics was more complex than that of Marcion, and also more subtle: they were able to interpret the Scriptures of Israel according to their own distinct viewpoints. Yet as far as the relationship between Israel and their communities of Christ believers was concerned, the result was similar. The God of Israel, whom the Jews believed to be the only god, was in fact a lesser deity, distinct from the supreme god for whom Christ served as emissary. The groups identified with these two deities stood in an analogous relationship: those who believed in Christ were totally separate from, and superior to, the people of Israel.

Over against Jewish Christians on one side, and Marcion and the Gnostics on the other, catholic Christianity defined itself in a two-fold way. First, as early as Justin's *Dialogue with Trypho the Jew* (*c.*155 CE), the Church claimed to be 'the true spiritual Israel' (11.5), the real 'religious and righteous nation' that God promised to Abraham (119.6). Thus, everything that was positive in Israel's tradition now was taken over by the Church, including the Scriptures, which are no longer 'yours, but ours' (29.2). Second, they claimed that Israel's Scriptures pointed ahead to Christ, who represents their true meaning and with whose coming the law, with its specific injunctions (circumcision, food laws, sacrifice, and so on), has come to an end.

Some versions of this self-definition can be described simply as supersessionist: the Church is a new entity that, with the coming of Christ, has supplanted and replaced the old. Justin, for example, sees the Church as the people of the promised 'new covenant' (*Dialogue* 11.4–5) and thus as a new Israel. For Tertullian, just as Jacob supplanted his elder brother Esau, so the Christians have supplanted the Jews as God's people (*Answer to the Jews* 1.3–6). Accordingly, Christ has abolished what is old and has established something new – a 'new law', replacing the old (3.8–10); spiritual circumcision, replacing the circumcision of the flesh (3.11); a sabbath that is eternal, replacing one that was temporal (4.2–3); spiritual sacrifices, replacing those that were earthly and carnal (5.1–7); a new kingdom, replacing the corruptible kingdoms of Solomon and other earthly rulers (6.3). In this view of things, a primary reason for this replacement of the old with the new (i.e. supersession) was Israel's sinfulness. While it was believed that this sinfulness was definitively expressed in their rejection of Christ, it is also part of a pattern that stretches back to the incident of the golden calf (Exod. 32; see Justin, *Dialogue* 131.3—132.1; Tertullian, *Answer to the Jews* 1.6–8; 3.13).

Such an understanding of Christian identity, based on ideas of promise and fulfilment or rejection and replacement, overlaps to a considerable extent with patterns already present in New Testament writings. But in the world of Justin and Tertullian this approach created problems. On one side, the Romans placed a high value on ancestral tradition. While they often found the Jews to be perplexingly different, they were at least prepared to concede that Jewish difference was based on long-standing customs. It was no accident that Josephus, in addressing the Roman world in his apologetic account of Jewish history, called his work 'the history of our antiquities' (*Against Apion* 1.1). On another side, the Greek philosophic tradition, which Justin and others wanted to use in support of their Christian claim, had come to conceive of the ultimate deity as unchanging, consistent and constant. In such an environment, to describe the Church as a *new* Israel, constituted by a *new* covenant, following a *new* law, and so on, was to concede a certain priority to the Jews and to suggest that God was fickle and changeable (see *Dialogue* 23, 30). If the Church is a *new* Israel, does this not mean that the Jews have ancestral tradition on their side? Why should God establish one people, covenant and law only to replace them with another? Perceptive outsiders, such as the Greek writer Celsus who wrote a whole treatise in criticism of the Christians (*The True Doctrine*, *c.*175 CE), were quick to pick this up, and even to use Jewish viewpoints to undermine Christian claims.

And so Justin and other Gentile Christians took an additional step, developing the idea that Israel's Scripture was a Christian book not simply in that it pointed ahead to Christ, but in that this deeper spiritual and christological meaning should have been readily apparent all along. It was only because of their excessive blindness and sinfulness that the Jews saw positive value in the literal observance of the laws of circumcision, sacrifice and so on. The only purpose served by the law in the literal sense was to curb Jewish sinfulness. As Justin says to Trypho: 'We too would observe your circumcision of the flesh, your Sabbath days, and, in a word, all your festivals, if we were not aware of the reason why they were imposed upon you, namely, because of your sins and your hardness of heart' (*Dialogue* 18.2). Instead, the true meaning of the law resided in its deeper, spiritual teachings about Christ, teachings – and this is an important point – that had been fully understood by the saints and righteous ones in Israel (*Dialogue* 40.1—42.4). Even before the time of Justin, the point had already been argued by Ignatius. For Ignatius, the reason that the prophets were persecuted was that they 'lived according to Jesus Christ' (*Magnesians* 8.2). Further, the prophets 'hoped in him [Jesus] and awaited him. And they were saved by believing in him, because they stood in the unity of Jesus Christ' (*Philadelphians* 5.2).

In this view, the Church is not really a 'new Israel' brought into being to replace the old. Instead it represents the continuation of a portion of Israel that had existed all along. Israel itself had always consisted of two parts – 'true Israel', who recognized the spiritual, Christ-centred meaning of Israel's Scriptures and institutions; and sinful Israel, who could not see beyond the literal sense and who persecuted those prophets and saints who could. The theme is strikingly illustrated in a passage from a third-century tractate 'against the Jews' attributed (falsely) to Cyprian, where scriptural figures are presented in contrasting pairs:

> Moses they cursed because he proclaimed Christ,
> Dathan they loved because he did not proclaim Him . . .
> David they hated because he sang of Christ,
> Saul they magnified because he did not speak of Him . . .
> Jeremiah they stoned while he was hymning Christ,
> Ananias they loved while he was opposing Him . . .[5]

It was in such a context and in support of such a definition of Christian identity that the New Testament came into existence as an authoritative collection of Christian Scripture.

Rhetorical function

Here we can be brief. At one level, the function of the New Testament as a canonical whole was the same as that of its component parts in their original contexts: to support, nurture and defend a specific community of believers by reinforcing their sense of identity and providing them with the resources needed to maintain their existence in an often threatening world. In the second- and third-century context, however, this sense of identity was shaped by factors that were not present (or were only beginning to emerge) in the first: the transformation of the movement into a Gentile entity; the need to

[5] Pseudo-Cyprian, *Adversus Judaeos* 3.3; cited by James Parkes, *The Conflict of the Church and the Synagogue: A Study in the Origins of Antisemitism* (New York: Atheneum, 1985), 105–6.

develop authority structures to defend the 'orthodox' Church from its 'heretical' competitors; and the need to redefine the Church's relationship to Israel and the Jews so that it would be able to win a sympathetic hearing from the larger non-Jewish world.

To sum up, it was in such a social context, in the service of such a pattern of self-definition and with such community-building needs in view that the New Testament came into being as a collected entity. Inevitably this had an effect on the way in which the New Testament, in its individual parts and as a scriptural whole, was understood and interpreted. Even if the 'anti-Judaic' material in the New Testament writings can be understood as originating in a context of dispute among different Jewish groups about the appropriate way to be Jewish, the same material, without any change in wording, readily became anti-Judaic in the Gentile context in which the canon was emerging. As Paula Fredriksen has put it, 'Jewish sectarian rhetoric, shorn of its native context, eventually became anti-Jewish rhetoric.'[6] Further, uncomfortable questions raised by Gentile outsiders concerning the relationship between the Church and Judaism meant that such anti-Jewish rhetoric became useful in a new way. Not simply a relic from the past, it had persuasive value in the present, as a means of distancing the Church from the Jews and deflecting the attacks of its critics. To win the Gentiles, Christian apologists felt it necessary to denigrate the Jews.

More generally, the fact that this collection came to be called the 'New Testament', and that it stood alongside the 'Old Testament' in a single canon of Christian Scripture, implied a particular status for the Scriptures of Israel and a particular relationship between the people of the one and that of the other. Further, it put the New Testament writings in a context that readily lent itself to ways of understanding the relationship between the two that went beyond that of a simple succession of 'old' and 'new', and that turned the anti-Judaic elements in these writings to much more malevolent ends. Perhaps most significantly, the fact that these writings came to constitute the canon of Gentile Christianity implicitly led Gentile believers to believe that these writings pertained to them simply and

[6] Paula Fredriksen, *Augustine and the Jews: A Christian Defense of Jews and Judaism* (New York: Doubleday, 2008), 82.

directly as Gentiles and as members of a Gentile Church. The context in which these writings functioned as Scripture obscured the fact that most of them were written by Jewish believers, and in a context where Jewish believers were the norm and Gentiles were the outsiders who had been drawn in.

To be sure, there is little evidence that the process of canon formation resulted in explicit changes to the content or wording of the New Testament writings. In addition, modern critical study has provided us with powerful tools that enable us to move behind the canon and to see these writings in their original contexts. Still, it requires considerable mental effort to carry this out and to read these texts in the way in which they would have been understood by the mixed communities of Jews and Gentiles to whom they were originally addressed. In other words, the context in which the New Testament came to be has had a lasting impact on the way in which it has been perceived and understood, even to the present day.

Interpreting the New Testament today

What, then, about the interpretation of the New Testament in our own day? Once again I will use the same three axes as I make a few concluding comments.

Social location

Interpretation is not a generic enterprise; it depends on a variety of things, especially the aims and identity of the interpreter. Some interpreters are interested in the New Testament as a historical source for the emergence of early Christianity, others as a classic of western culture and a seedbed for western literature, still others as a testing-ground for critical theory. In addition, there are many who have been wounded by the New Testament, who have experienced it as an instrument of oppression, exclusion or – to return to our point of departure with Jules Isaac – of antisemitism. Different interpreters are motivated by different questions, which results in different interpretations. Before the New Testament was of interest from any of these perspectives, however, it was – and continues to be – the Scripture of a living religion, and this is the community of interpreters that I choose to focus on here. What can be said about the interpretation of the New Testament, and in particular the elements of it that might be seen as anti-Judaic, within contemporary Christianity? While I identify myself as a Christian and thus see myself as someone engaged in this interpretive task, here I want to work in a slightly broader context. I am not writing specifically as a Christian to other Christians (though I hope that other Christians will be included among my readership). What I have to say here could just as easily be said by a sympathetic outsider, and addressed to other outsiders with a sympathetic interest in contemporary religion.

Here, then, I am interested in the interpretation of the New Testament in the context of contemporary western Christianity. The most important features of this context have been touched on already. As we have just observed, the foundations of western Christianity (including the canon of the New Testament itself) were laid in the second century, when the Church emerged as a distinctively Gentile institution. We began our study, however, with the Holocaust and the painful questions that were raised, by Jules Isaac and others, about the Church's complicity in this unthinkable event. Such questions led to a growing recognition of the ways in which anti-Jewish interpretation of the New Testament had contributed to a legacy of anti-Judaism and antisemitism within Christendom, which, in turn, had helped to create the environment in which the Nazi programme of genocide was carried out. We have seen how this anti-Jewish pattern of interpretation emerged in the second century, as part of a process of self-definition that involved the establishment of the New Testament canon itself.

In the first chapter we noted several additional factors at work in the social location of contemporary western Christianity. One is the waning of Christendom and the end of the Church's dominance in public life and social formation. While this has led to increasing secularization, the globalization of culture has also created an environment of religious pluralism, which has prodded the Church to be increasingly sensitive to the ways in which its own religious claims might be perceived as offending the rights and self-understanding of others. In addition, ongoing dialogue between Christians and Jews has increased Christian sensitivity to the ways in which Jews perceive the New Testament, just as new discoveries and scholarly insights have sharpened our perceptions of the Jewish environment within which Jesus carried out his ministry and the Christian movement began.

Rhetorical function

The role of the New Testament with respect to its present readers is similar to the role of the individual writings with respect to the original intended readers. These writings originated as instruments of community formation. That is, they were produced in order to provide early communities of believers with the foundations, structures and practical resources that would enable them to maintain their existence and carry out their mission in their own particular contexts. The formation of the New Testament canon has made it possible for these writings to continue to function in this way with subsequent generations of readers.

What, then, are contemporary readers to do with those New Testament texts and themes that seem to reflect negatively on Jews and Judaism? The answer to this question is to be found in the way in which the Church engages the process of Christian self-definition.

Self-definition

How, then, is the Church to understand and define itself in its present context? In posing the question, I make two assumptions. On the one hand, I am thinking here of a Church that is sensitive to the Church's legacy of supersessionism, anti-Judaism and antisemitism, and that desires a positive relationship with Judaism as a co-inhabitant of the contemporary religious landscape. On the other, I have in view a Church that wants to treat the New Testament with integrity as its canonical Scripture. How does one carry out a process of Christian self-definition that is faithful to the concerns and commitments on both sides?

I hasten to say that I am not going to attempt anything like a comprehensive answer. Constructive theology is a task that I am content to leave to those who are better equipped than I.[7] My contribution here is more narrowly restricted to the New Testament itself and to the place of New Testament interpretation in such an enterprise

[7] See e.g. R. Kendall Soulen, *The God of Israel and Christian Theology* (Minneapolis: Fortress Press, 1996); John Howard Yoder, *The Jewish–Christian Schism Revisited*, ed. Michael G. Cartwright and Peter Ochs (Grand Rapids: Eerdmans, 2003); Carl E. Braaten and Robert W. Jenson (eds), *Jews and Christians: People of God* (Grand Rapids: Eerdmans, 2003).

of self-definition. It will take the form of a series of statements with comment.

1. In one way or another, the writings of the New Testament all ascribe ultimate significance to Christ.

While there is considerable diversity in the New Testament (on which more in a moment), the individual writings agree in their presentation of Jesus as a figure of universal significance. He is the one to whom 'all authority in heaven and earth has been given' (Matt. 28.18 NRSV), the only 'way . . . to the Father' (John 14.6), 'the one ordained by God as judge of the living and the dead' (Acts 10.42 NRSV), the one who 'has died for all' (2 Cor. 5.14), the Lord, at whose name 'every knee should bend, in heaven and on earth and under the earth' (Phil. 2.10–11 NRSV), 'the Saviour of all people' (1 Tim. 4.10 NRSV), the 'Son, whom [God] appointed heir of all things' (Heb. 1.2 NRSV). In his titles and roles, and in what he has accomplished, Jesus is ascribed ultimate and universal significance.

2. In one way or another, the writings of the New Testament present Christ's person and work as the goal and culmination of the story of Israel.

'Christ died for our sins in accordance with the scriptures,' Paul says in one of the earliest summaries of what he and other early Christians called 'the gospel' (1 Cor. 15.3 NRSV). The longer versions of the message in Acts are studded with scriptural citations, all in service of the argument that 'what God promised to our ancestors he has fulfilled for us, their children, by raising Jesus' (Acts 13.32–33 NRSV). This theme represents a major plot element in the stories of Jesus in the Gospels, and is reiterated throughout the rest of the New Testament.

3. These two claims about Christ stand in considerable tension with the Jewish understanding of how the story of Israel would reach its goal and culmination.

While the terms in which the Christian message was presented – kingdom of God, Messiah/Christ, fulfilment of God's promises, salvation, and so on – would have been fully recognizable to Jewish ears, the message itself would have been puzzling at best. Jewish expectations about the promised age of salvation did not contain any notion of a Messiah who would suffer and die, who would do so as a means of bringing salvation, but who would be removed to heaven without having established the expected era of righteousness under the reign of God. Jewish expectation centred much more on the coming *age* than on the human *agent* who would bring it about; thus, the idea of a Messiah without a messianic age would have appeared as a virtual contradiction in terms. While there is a definite logic to the early claims about Christ if one begins with the belief that God raised the crucified Messiah from the dead, such an event was unanticipated in Jewish expectation. In other words, some element of tension between Christian claim and Jewish expectation is inevitable in any form of self-definition based on the New Testament.

4. New Testament claims about the significance of Christ are qualified by the expectation that his accomplishments will be brought to completion only with his 'coming' in the future.

In Luke's words, the 'time of universal restoration that God announced long ago through his holy prophets' will fully arrive only at the appointed time in the future when God sends 'the Messiah appointed for you, that is, Jesus' (Acts 3.20–21 NRSV). Christ's resurrection is just the 'first fruits' of the more general resurrection to be experienced 'at his coming' by 'those who belong to Christ,' says Paul in 1 Corinthians 15.23, going on to add 'then comes the end'. To use a common formulation, the salvation accomplished by Christ is both 'already' and 'not yet'; aspects of it are experienced in the present, but the full experience will take place only in the future.

In a real sense, then, the tension between Christian claim and Jewish expectation is not an external thing but is intrinsic to the Christian claim itself. Christians themselves experience the tension between their belief in a universal saviour and the all-too-apparent reality of a world in which signs of salvation are few and far between. The Christian message that 'the saviour has come' is at the same time the message that 'this is the saviour who will come'. The message concerning the fulfilment of God's promises of salvation is also a message about God's unfinished business. The first part of the message differentiates Christian from Jew, and opens up a space of disputed territory between them. The second part, however, puts them on shared ground – the hopeful expectation that the age of salvation promised by the God of Israel will be fully established in the future. While this does not by itself resolve the tensions between Christian claim and Jewish expectation, it at least puts them into a framework in which they might be managed.

5. There is an ethical element in the process of interpretation; interpreters need to take responsibility for the decisions they make.

Any interpreter of New Testament texts is faced with decisions that need to be made about the meaning and significance of various textual aspects. As we have seen, this is true in particular with respect to New Testament texts pertaining to Jews and Judaism. Each of the writings that we have investigated presents us with whole sets of related questions; decisions made at each point accumulate, resulting in a considerable range of interpretations, some much more anti-Judaic than others. Interpretation, then, is neither a mechanical nor an innocent act; it results from a set of conscious decisions, for which interpreters need to take responsibility. I am not suggesting here that interpreters should necessarily choose a more benign interpretation over one that is more harmful or malevolent; if one is convinced that Matthew intended the cry of 'all the people' in 27.25 ('his blood be on us and on our children') to signal the final dereliction of Israel, then this is the interpretation that one needs to make. Nevertheless, in arriving at such an interpretation one also needs to recognize that interpretations about texts can have – indeed, have had – consequences in the real world, which means that interpreters have a responsibility to consider the ends to which their interpretations might be put. There is an ethical dimension to the task of interpretation.

6. Contemporary Christians need to read the New Testament as Gentile Christians.

The New Testament canon emerged in a Church that had become almost exclusively Gentile and, more importantly, that defined itself by its perceived contrast with 'the Jews'. This naturally led to the assumption on the part of Gentile Christians that the writings of the New Testament were addressed to them directly and exclusively. Put differently, the assumption was – and continues to be – that the New Testament writings are addressed simply to Christians as an undifferentiated group, so that any distinctions that might be made within these writings between Jews and Gentiles are incidental and of no ongoing significance.

As we have seen, however, such distinctions were a fundamental part of the social world in which the New Testament writings emerged. Many of the intended readers of these writings were Jewish. All of them recognized that the Christian movement began as a Jewish entity and that the admission of Gentiles was a subsequent development, involving controversy and difference of opinion over the terms of admission. In some measure, the world reflected in the New Testament writings is one in which Gentile Christians represent a special case rather than the norm. Of course, this world no longer exists. The wild olive shoots have now taken over the tree (cf. Rom. 11.17–21); the special case has become the norm. But Paul's call for Gentile humility still stands. In reading the New Testament and forming their own identity, contemporary Christians should begin by identifying themselves with the Gentiles in the text, those special-case Christians who have been invited in to share in the 'spiritual blessings' that belong in the first instance to Jews (cf. Rom. 15.27).

7. Christian interpretation of the New Testament should be carried out in dialogue with Jewish interpreters.

As we have observed, for the past century Jewish scholars have increasingly become interested in the New Testament and in studying Christian origins as an aspect of the history of Judaism. Christian interpretation of the New Testament has consequently been enriched, corrected and improved, a fact that has been readily apparent in the preceding pages of this book. In the process of drawing on the New Testament to shape Christian identity in the present context, Christian interpreters have much to learn by carrying out their task in dialogue with their Jewish counterparts and colleagues. If such dialogue is carried out in the proper spirit, it will produce a Christian self-understanding characterized by greater integrity and a more humble stance towards its religious neighbours.

8. Christian interpretation of the New Testament should be fully aware of the history of scriptural interpretation, especially as it pertains to Jews and Judaism.

With the work of James Parkes, Jules Isaac, Rosemary Ruether and others, the post-Holocaust search for causes has made us aware of the role played by biblical interpretation in the development of anti-Judaic attitudes among Christians and in Christian tradition. To avoid unexamined assumptions and unidentified blind-spots, Christian interpreters should be thoroughly familiar with this history. While this history is full of negative examples and cautionary tales, interpreters should also be prepared to look for more positive models and constructive patterns of interpretation. Paula Fredriksen's recent book on Augustine is a good case in point.[8]

9. The canon of the New Testament offers more options for Christian self-definition than were held by those involved in the process of canonization.

The first two statements in this list drew attention to some core beliefs that (in my opinion) were held in common by the authors of New Testament writings. The other side of this coin, however, is the considerable variety within these writings both in the way these beliefs are expressed and in the way in which their theological implications are explored and developed. The core message – that God was fulfilling the prophetic promises of salvation by raising Jesus from the dead – brought with it as many questions as answers. (i) Who is Jesus, that his life, death and resurrection should have such far-reaching consequences? (ii) How is it that the life, death and resurrection of the Messiah should bring salvation? What is the problem for which this is the divinely provided solution? (iii) What is the nature of the present period (between the resurrection of the Messiah and the parousia) and how is it related to the past (the story of Israel) and the future (the full establishment of God's reign with the parousia of the Messiah)? (iv) What is the relationship between the new

[8] *Augustine and the Jews.*

people of the Messiah and the original people of Israel, on the one hand, and the larger world of the Gentiles, on the other?

For our purposes, the most significant question is the fourth, though the others are pertinent as well. These questions were not immediately resolved; indeed, Christians have continued to wrestle with them (along with others) right up to the present. This process of theological development is readily apparent in the writings of the New Testament. In addition, the New Testament contains considerable variety in the way these questions are addressed and in the answers that are proposed. We have certainly seen this to be the case in the issues of Christian self-definition that we have explored in preceding chapters. While the Gentile Church in which the canon was produced had arrived at a particular formulation of self-definition, the writings that were canonized contained a broader diversity. While it is not possible to repeal history and return to an earlier era, it is nevertheless the case that the phenomenon of diversity within the New Testament canon provides resources for continuing the process of Christian self-definition in the present.

10. The New Testament provides us with examples of living with tension.

Finally, contemporary Christians are not the first to experience unresolved tensions. The most poignant New Testament example is found in Paul's epistle to the Romans. The logic of Paul's argument up to chapter 11 might seem to suggest that the story of his 'kindred according to the flesh' (9.3) had run its course and come to an end. But at this point Paul shows himself prepared to live with unresolved tension rather than to sacrifice his people and God's promises to the logic of his argument. God's judgements may be 'inscrutable' (11.33) but after Paul has done his best to search them out he is content in the end to leave it to God to deal with God's own unfinished business. The Church in our own day may be well advised to do the same.

Bibliography

Balch, David L. (ed.). *Social History of the Matthean Community: Cross-Disciplinary Approaches* (Minneapolis: Fortress Press, 1991).

Barrett, C. K. *A Critical and Exegetical Commentary on the Acts of the Apostles*, vol. 2 (Edinburgh: T&T Clark, 1998).

Bauckham, Richard. *The Testimony of the Beloved Disciple: Narrative, History, and Theology in the Gospel of John* (Grand Rapids: Baker Academic, 2007).

Bauckham, Richard (ed.). *The Gospels for All Christians: Rethinking the Gospel Audiences* (Grand Rapids: Eerdmans, 1998).

Baum, Gregory. *Is the New Testament Anti-Semitic? A Re-Examination of the New Testament* (Glen Rock, NJ: Paulist Press, 1965).

——*The Jews and the Gospel: A Re-Examination of the New Testament* (Westminster, Md.: Newman Press, 1961).

Baur, F. C. *Paul: The Apostle of Jesus Christ* (London: Williams & Norgate, 1876).

Becker, Adam H., and Annette Yoshiko Reed (eds). *The Ways That Never Parted: Jews and Christians in Late Antiquity and the Early Middle Ages* (Minneapolis: Fortress Press, 2007).

Boyarin, Daniel. *Border Lines: The Partition of Judaeo-Christianity* (Philadelphia: University of Pennsylvania Press, 2004).

Braaten, Carl E., and Robert W. Jenson (eds). *Jews and Christians: People of God* (Grand Rapids: Eerdmans, 2003).

Brawley, Robert L. *Luke–Acts and the Jews: Conflict, Apology, and Conciliation* (Atlanta, Ga.: Scholars Press, 1987).

Brown, Raymond E. *The Community of the Beloved Disciple* (New York: Paulist Press, 1979).

——*The Gospel According to John*, 2 vols, Anchor Bible (Garden City, NY: Doubleday, 1966 and 1970).

Bruce, F. F. *Commentary on the Book of the Acts* (Grand Rapids: Eerdmans, 1975).

Cargal, Timothy B. '"His Blood be Upon Us and Upon Our Children": A Matthean Double Entendre?' *New Testament Studies* 37 (1991): 101–12.

Clark, Kenneth W. 'The Gentile Bias in Matthew', *Journal of Biblical Literature* 66 (1947): 165–72.

Culpepper, R. Alan. 'Anti-Judaism in the Fourth Gospel as a Theological Problem for Christian Interpreters', in *Anti-Judaism and the Fourth Gospel*, ed. R. Bieringer, D. Pollefeyt and F. Vandecasteele-Vanneuville, 61–82 (Louisville, Ky.: Westminster John Knox Press, 2001).

Davies, Alan T. (ed.). *Antisemitism and the Foundations of Christianity* (New York and Toronto: Paulist Press, 1979).

Davies, W. D. *Paul and Rabbinic Judaism* (London: SPCK, 1948).

Dennis, John A. *Jesus' Death and the Gathering of True Israel: The Johannine Appropriation of Restoration Theology in the Light of John 11.47–52*, WUNT 2/217 (Tübingen: Mohr Siebeck, 2006).

Donaldson, Terence L. 'Introduction to the Pauline Corpus', in *The Oxford Bible Commentary*, ed. John Barton and John Muddiman, 1062–83 (Oxford: Oxford University Press, 2001).

——*Jesus on the Mountain: A Study in Matthean Theology* (Sheffield: JSOT Press, 1985).

——'Jewish Christianity, Israel's Stumbling and the *Sonderweg* Reading of Paul', *Journal for the Study of the New Testament* 29 (2006): 27–54.

——*Judaism and the Gentiles: Jewish Patterns of Universalism (to 135 CE)* (Waco, Tex.: Baylor University Press, 2007).

——*Paul and the Gentiles: Remapping the Apostle's Convictional World* (Minneapolis: Fortress Press, 1997).

Dunn, James D. G. 'An Embarrassment of History: Reflections on the Problem of "Anti-Judaism" in the Fourth Gospel', in *Anti-Judaism and the Fourth Gospel*, ed. R. Bieringer, D. Pollefeyt and F. Vandecasteele-Vanneuville, 41–60 (Louisville, Ky.: Westminster John Knox Press, 2001).

——'The New Perspective on Paul', *Bulletin of the John Rylands Library* 65 (1983): 95–122.

——*The New Perspective on Paul*, rev. edn (Grand Rapids: Eerdmans, 2005).

——*The Partings of the Ways Between Christianity and Judaism and Their Significance for the Character of Christianity* (London: SCM Press; Philadelphia: Trinity Press International, 1991).

——*The Theology of Paul the Apostle* (Edinburgh: T&T Clark, 1997; Grand Rapids: Eerdmans, 1998).

Dunn, James D. G. (ed.). *Jews and Christians: The Parting of the Ways, A.D. 70 to 135* (Grand Rapids: Eerdmans, 1999).

Flannery, Edward H. *The Anguish of the Jews: Twenty-Three Centuries of Anti-Semitism* (New York: Macmillan, 1965).

——'Anti-Judaism and Anti-Semitism: A Necessary Distinction', *Journal of Ecumenical Studies* 10 (1973): 581–8.

Fredriksen, Paula. *Augustine and the Jews: A Christian Defense of Jews and Judaism* (New York: Doubleday, 2008).

Gager, John G. *The Origins of Anti-Semitism* (Oxford: Oxford University Press, 1983).

——*Reinventing Paul* (Oxford: Oxford University Press, 2000).

Garland, David E. *The Intention of Matthew 23*, Supplements to *Novum Testamentum* 52 (Leiden: Brill, 1979).

Gaston, Lloyd. 'Anti-Judaism and the Passion Narrative in Luke and Acts', in *Anti-Judaism in Early Christianity*, vol. 1: *Paul and the Gospels*, ed. Peter Richardson with David Granskou, 127–53 (Waterloo, Ont.: Wilfrid Laurier University Press, 1986).

——'The Messiah of Israel as Teacher of the Gentiles: The Setting of Matthew's Christology', *Interpretation* 29 (1975): 24–40.

——'Paul and the Torah', in *Antisemitism and the Foundations of Christianity*, ed. Alan T. Davies, 48–71 (New York and Toronto: Paulist Press, 1979).

Haenchen, Ernst. *The Acts of the Apostles: A Commentary* (Oxford: Blackwell, 1971).

——'The Book of Acts as Source Material for the History of Early Christianity', in *Studies in Luke–Acts*, ed. Leander E. Keck and J. Louis Martyn, 258–78 (Minneapolis: Augsburg, 1966).

Hare, Douglas R. A. 'The Rejection of the Jews in the Synoptic Gospels and Acts', in *Antisemitism and the Foundations of Christianity*, ed. Alan T. Davies, 27–47 (New York and Toronto: Paulist Press, 1979).

——*The Theme of Jewish Persecution of Christians in the Gospel According to St. Matthew*, Society for New Testament Studies Monograph Series 6 (Cambridge: Cambridge University Press, 1967).

Hare, Douglas R. A., and Daniel J. Harrington. '"Make Disciples of All the Gentiles" (Mt 28.19)', *Catholic Biblical Quarterly* 37 (1975): 359–69.

Isaac, Jules. *Jesus and Israel* (New York: Holt, Rinehart & Winston, 1971).

——*Jésus et Israël* (Paris: Albin Michel, 1948).

——*The Teaching of Contempt: Christian Roots of Anti-Semitism* (New York: Holt, Rinehart & Winston, 1964).

Jervell, Jacob. 'The Church of Jews and Godfearers', in *Luke–Acts and the Jewish People*, ed. Joseph B. Tyson, 11–20 (Minneapolis: Augsburg, 1988).

——*Luke and the People of God* (Minneapolis: Augsburg, 1972).

Johnson, Luke Timothy. 'The New Testament's Anti-Jewish Slander and the Conventions of Ancient Polemic', *Journal of Biblical Literature* 108 (1989): 419–41.

Jossa, Giorgio. *Jews or Christians? The Followers of Jesus in Search of Their Own Identity*, WUNT 1/202 (Tübingen: Mohr Siebeck, 2006).

Kierspel, Lars. *The Jews and the World in the Fourth Gospel: Parallelism, Function, and Context*, WUNT 2/220 (Tübingen: Mohr Siebeck, 2006).

Kim, Lloyd. *Polemic in the Book of Hebrews: Anti-Semitism, Anti-Judaism, Supersessionism?* Princeton Theological Monograph Series (Eugene, Or.: Pickwick, 2006).

Koenig, John. *Jews and Christians in Dialogue: New Testament Foundations* (Philadelphia: Westminster Press, 1979).

Koester, Helmut. *Introduction to the New Testament*, vol. 2: *History and Literature of Early Christianity* (Philadelphia: Fortress Press, 1982).

Lieu, Judith. '"The Parting of the Ways": Theological Construct or Historical Reality?' *Journal for the Study of the New Testament* 56 (1994): 101–19.

Littell, Franklin H. *The Crucifixion of the Jews* (New York: Harper & Row, 1975).

Lovsky, Fadiey. *Antisémitisme et mystère d'Israël* (Paris: A. Michel, 1955).

Lowe, Malcolm F. 'Who Were the Ioudaioi?' *Novum Testamentum* 18 (1976): 101–30.

Martyn, J. Louis. *History and Theology in the Fourth Gospel* (New York: Harper & Row, 1968).

Mayo, Philip L. *'Those Who Call Themselves Jews': The Church and Judaism in the Apocalypse of John*, Princeton Theological Monograph Series (Eugene, Or.: Pickwick, 2006).

Meier, John P. 'Nations or Gentiles in Matthew 28.19?' *Catholic Biblical Quarterly* 39 (1977): 94–102.

Moessner, David P. 'The Ironic Fulfilment of Israel's Glory', in *Luke–Acts and the Jewish People*, ed. Joseph B. Tyson, 35–50 (Minneapolis: Augsburg, 1988).

Montefiore, C. G. *Judaism and St. Paul: Two Essays* (London: Max Goschen, 1914).

Motyer, Stephen. 'The Fourth Gospel and the Salvation of Israel: An Appeal for a New Start', in *Anti-Judaism and the Fourth Gospel*, ed. R. Bieringer, D. Pollefeyt and F. Vandecasteele-Vanneuville, 83–100 (Louisville, Ky.: Westminster John Knox Press, 2001).

Munck, Johannes. *Paul and the Salvation of Mankind* (London: SCM Press, 1959).

Nanos, Mark D. *The Mystery of Romans: The Jewish Context of Paul's Letter* (Minneapolis: Fortress Press, 1996).

Overman, J. Andrew. *Matthew's Gospel and Formative Judaism: The Social World of the Matthean Community* (Minneapolis: Fortress Press, 1990).

Paley, William. *Horæ Paulinæ* (London: Printed by J. Davis, for R. Faulder, 1790).

Parkes, James. *The Conflict of the Church and the Synagogue: A Study in the Origins of Antisemitism* (London: Soncino Press, 1934).

——*Jesus, Paul and the Jews* (London: SCM Press, 1936).

——*The Jew and His Neighbour: A Study of the Causes of Anti-Semitism* (London: SCM Press, 1930).

Reinhartz, Adele. '"Jews" and Jews in the Fourth Gospel', in *Anti-Judaism and the Fourth Gospel*, ed. R. Bieringer, D. Pollefeyt and F. Vandecasteele-Vanneuville, 213–27 (Louisville, Ky.: Westminster John Knox Press, 2001).

Rensberger, David. 'Anti-Judaism and the Gospel of John', in *Anti-Judaism and the Gospels*, ed. William Reuben Farmer, 120–57 (Harrisburg, Pa.: Trinity Press International, 1999).

Robinson, John A. T. *Twelve New Testament Studies* (Naperville, Ill.: Allenson, 1962).

Ruether, Rosemary R. *Faith and Fratricide: The Theological Roots of Anti-Semitism* (Minneapolis: Seabury, 1974).

Saldarini, Anthony J. *Matthew's Christian-Jewish Community* (Chicago: University of Chicago Press, 1994).

Sanders, E. P. *Paul and Palestinian Judaism* (Philadelphia: Fortress Press, 1977).

——*Paul, the Law, and the Jewish People* (Philadelphia: Fortress Press, 1983).

Sanders, Jack T. *The Jews in Luke–Acts* (Philadelphia: Fortress Press, 1987).

——'The Jews in Luke–Acts', in *Luke–Acts and the Jewish People*, ed. Joseph B. Tyson, 51–75 (Minneapolis: Augsburg, 1988).

Schoeps, Hans-Joachim. *Paul: The Theology of the Apostle in the Light of Jewish Religious History* (Philadelphia: Westminster Press, 1961).

Schweitzer, Albert. *The Mysticism of Paul the Apostle* (London: A&C Black, 1931).

Segal, Alan F. *Paul the Convert: The Apostolate and Apostasy of Saul the Pharisee* (New Haven: Yale University Press, 1990).

Sim, David C. *The Gospel of Matthew and Christian Judaism: The History and Social Setting of the Matthean Community* (Edinburgh: T&T Clark, 1998).

Simon, Marcel. *Verus Israel: A Study of the Relations Between Christians and Jews in the Roman Empire (135–425)* (New York: Oxford University Press for the Littman Library, 1986).

Smiga, George M. *Pain and Polemic: Anti-Judaism in the Gospels* (New York: Paulist Press, 1992).

Soulen, R. Kendall. *The God of Israel and Christian Theology* (Minneapolis: Fortress Press, 1996).

Stanton, Graham N. *A Gospel for a New People: Studies in Matthew* (Louisville, Ky.: Westminster John Knox Press, 1993).

Stendahl, Krister. *Paul Among Jews and Gentiles* (Philadelphia: Fortress Press, 1976).

Sterling, Gregory E. *Historiography and Self-Definition: Josephos, Luke–Acts, and Apologetic Historiography*, Supplements to *Novum Testamentum* 64 (Leiden and New York: Brill, 1992).

Stowers, Stanley K. *A Rereading of Romans: Justice, Jews, and Gentiles* (New Haven: Yale University Press, 1994).

Tannehill, Robert C. 'Israel in Luke–Acts: A Tragic Story', *Journal of Biblical Literature* 104 (1985): 69–85.

——*The Narrative Unity of Luke–Acts: A Literary Interpretation*, 2 vols (Philadelphia: Fortress Press, 1986–90).

——'Rejection by Jews and Turning to Gentiles: The Pattern of Paul's Mission in Acts', in *Luke–Acts and the Jewish People*, ed. Joseph B. Tyson, 83–101 (Minneapolis: Augsburg, 1988).

Tiede, David L. '"Glory to Thy People Israel": Luke–Acts and the Jews', in *Luke–Acts and the Jewish People*, ed. Joseph B. Tyson, 21–34 (Minneapolis: Augsburg, 1988).

——*Prophecy and History in Luke–Acts* (Philadelphia: Fortress Press, 1980).

Tomson, Peter J. '"Jews" in the Gospel of John as Compared with the Palestinian Talmud, the Synoptics, and Some New Testament Apocrypha', in *Anti-Judaism and the Fourth Gospel*, ed. R. Bieringer, D. Pollefeyt and F. Vandecasteele-Vanneuville, 176–212 (Louisville, Ky.: Westminster John Knox Press, 2001).

Townsend, John. 'The Gospel of John and the Jews: The Story of a Religious Divorce', in *Antisemitism and the Foundations of Christianity*, ed. Alan T. Davies, 72–97 (New York and Toronto: Paulist Press, 1979).

Tyson, Joseph B. 'The Problem of Jewish Rejection in Acts', in *Luke–Acts and the Jewish People*, ed. Joseph B. Tyson, 124–37 (Minneapolis: Augsburg, 1988).

Westerholm, Stephen. *Perspectives Old and New on Paul: The 'Lutheran' Paul and His Critics* (Grand Rapids: Eerdmans, 2004).

Wrede, William. *Paul* (London: Green, 1907).

Wright, N. T. *The Climax of the Covenant: Christ and the Law in Pauline Theology* (Edinburgh: T&T Clark; Minneapolis: Fortress Press, 1991).

Yoder, John Howard. *The Jewish–Christian Schism Revisited*, ed. Michael G. Cartwright and Peter Ochs (Grand Rapids: Eerdmans, 2003).

Zoccali, Christopher. '"And So All Israel Will be Saved": Competing Interpretations of Romans 11.26 in Pauline Scholarship', *Journal for the Study of the New Testament* 30 (2008): 289–318.

Index of ancient sources

Acts

Index of modern authors